A Beginner's Guide to the iPhone

Books by the Same Author

Only a small selection of the total number of books published are listed below.

BP762	Microsoft Office 2016 Explained
BP757	Windows 10 Explained
BP743	Kindle Fire HDX Explained
BP738	Google for the Older Generation
BP284	Programming in QuickBASIC
BP259	A Concise Introduction to UNIX
BP258	Learning to Program in C
BP250	Programming in Fortran 77

Books Written with Phil Oliver

BP726	Microsoft Excel 2010 Explained
BP719	Microsoft Office 2010 Explained
BP710	An Introduction to Windows Live Essentials
BP590	Microsoft Access 2007 Explained
BP555	Using PDF Files
BP545	Paint Shop Pro 8 Explained
BP498	Using Visual Basic
BP341	MS-DOS Explained

A Beginner's Guide to the iPhone

by

Noel Kantaris

Bernard Babani (publishing) Ltd
The Grampians
Shepherds Bush Road
London W6 7NF
England

www.babanibooks.com

Please Note

Although every care has been taken with the production of this book to ensure that all information is correct at the time of writing and that any projects, designs, modifications and/or programs, etc., contained herewith, operate in a correct and safe manner and also that any components specified are normally available in Great Britain, the Publishers and Author(s) do not accept responsibility in any way for the failure (including fault in design) of any project, design, modification or program to work correctly or to cause damage to any equipment that it may be connected to or used in conjunction with, or in respect of any other damage or injury that may be so caused, nor do the Publishers accept responsibility in any way for the failure to obtain specified components.

Notice is also given that if equipment that is still under warranty is modified in any way or used or connected with home-built equipment then that warranty may be void.

British Library Cataloguing in Publication Data:

A catalogue record for this book is available from the British Library

ISBN 978 0 85934 783 9

Printed and bound in Great Britain for
Bernard Babani (publishing) Ltd

About this Book

A Beginner's Guide to the iPhone was written to help users get to grips with the various aspects of Apple's iPhone. Although there are several versions of the iPhone, its basic use, such as making and receiving calls, reading and sending texts, taking photos or downloading and installing new apps, remain the same on all versions of the iPhone.

You can also use the iPhone to send and receive e-mail messages with attachments which are free from a Wi-Fi connection or browse the Internet. The book also shows you how to keep information on your friends and family, using the built-in Contacts app and the equally useful Calendar app which help you to remember birthdays and appointments. The book covers a lot more than the basic usage of the iPhone.

So, whether you are an iPhone owner who would like to know more on what you can do with it or you are a total beginner who would like to learn its basic use (Apple does not supply a printed user guide with it), then this beginner's guide is ideal for you.

The material in this book is presented using simple language and avoiding technical jargon as much as possible. The book was written with the non technical person in mind, so its structure is based on 'what you need to know first, appears first'.

No prior knowledge of the iPhone is assumed, but more experienced users don't have to start at the beginning and go right through to the end, as the chapters have been designed to be fairly self-contained.

It is hoped that with the help of this book, you will be able to come to terms with the iPhone in the shortest, most effective and enjoyable way. Have fun!

Please Note: Most topics discussed in this book regarding the **iPhone**, are also equally applicable to the **iPad**, as both (up to now) are using the same Operating System (iOS). However, there are two differences between the two; you cannot make or receive telephone calls on the iPad even if it is equipped with a SIM, and as the size of the iPad screen is so much larger than that of the iPhone, certain tools and icons are sometimes positioned in different places (top or bottom) on the iPad.

This book has been checked on an iPhone 7 running iOS12.4 as well as iOS13 when it was updated. Further, it was also checked on iPhones 4S, 5S and SE. Any differences due to a different iOS running on these devices has been indicated throughout the text.

As the book is intended for beginners, covering the basic operation and functions it should also be compatible with later model iPhones, although screen displays could be a little different.

About the Author

Graduated in Electrical Engineering at Bristol University and after spending three years in the Electronics Industry in London, took up a Tutorship in Physics at the University of Queensland. Research interests in Ionospheric Physics, led to the degrees of M.E. in Electronics and Ph.D. in Physics. On return to the UK, he took up a Post-Doctoral Research Fellowship in Radio Physics at the University of Leicester, and then a lecturing position in Engineering at the Camborne School of Mines, Cornwall, (part of Exeter University), where he was also the CSM Computing Manager until retirement.

Acknowledgements

Thanks to friends for their helpful tips and suggestions which assisted me in writing this book. Also special thanks are due to my Publisher for encouraging me to wait for the release of the latest iPhone Operating System (iOS13), so that it could be incorporated in this book.

Trademarks

Dropbox is a registered trademark of Dropbox Inc.

iPlayer is a registered trademark of British Broadcasting Corporation.

IPad and **iPhone** are registered trademarks of Apple Inc.

iOS is an operating system used for Apple's mobile devices and is a registered trademark of Apple Inc.

Google is a registered trademark of Google Inc.

OneDrive is a registered trademark of Microsoft Inc.

Postscript is a registered trademark of Adobe Systems Inc.

WhatsApp is a registered trademark of Facebook Inc.

All other brand and product names used in the book are recognised as trademarks, or registered trademarks, of their respective companies.

Contents

1

Overview of the iPhone

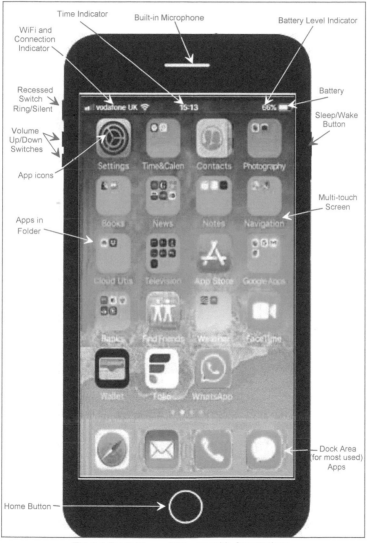

Fig.1.1 Front View of iPhone with Annotations.

The position of the 'Sleep/Wake' button, shown in Fig. 1.1, is for the iPhone 6 and later versions, while for earlier models this switch is to be found at the top-right side of the phone.

The view from the bottom of the iPhone is shown below:

Fig. 1.2 Bottom View of the iPhone.

In the middle of Fig. 1.2 is the charging port (this is more elongated for iPhones prior to version 5). On either side of it, a built-in microphone is to be found (square shapes above), while the round shapes represent built-in stereo speakers.

Starting the iPhone

When you first start a new iPhone for the very first time, you are asked to plug it into a power socket, using the connecting cable provided, so it can be charged up.

Following this, the iPhone loads the Setup Assistant which:

- Senses the presence of your 'Wi-Fi' and asks you for the required key (usually to be found on the back of your router) to make the connection to your home network, as shown in Fig. 1.3. Note the displayed on-screen keyboard which you use to enter your 'WiFi' password which is case sensitive, so be careful!

- Next, the Assistant asks you to create an 'Apple ID', usually your e-mail address with a password.

Fig. 1.3 Connecting to WiFi.

Apple likes you to create a password which includes a mixture of capital and lower case letters plus a few numbers. It is a good idea to create a password that is simple and you can remember it easily, as you'll be asked for it frequently. You might also be asked to provide details of a card so you can create an account with the **Apple Store** and **iTunes**, to purchase apps, music, etc.

- Finally, the Assistant asks you to join 'iCloud' - a storage facility of 5 GByte free capacity where you can keep your Calendar, Contacts and Photos - this can be increased to 50 GBytes for a very modest fee of 79 pence a month (at the time of writing), but will not be needed until your photos exceed more than a thousand. Use the same ID and password as the Apple ID and password.

Using the iPhone to Communicate

The very first thing you would want to use the iPhone for is to make or receive a phone call.

Making a call

To make a call using an iPhone to a person in your contacts list:

- Tap the **Contacts** app icon on the 'Home' screen (I am using an iPhone 7, so the image on the icon might be a bit different for

  you), to open a list of contacts as in Fig. 1.4 (see Chapter 3 on how to create such a list).

- Scroll down to the person you want to call and tap their name to display what information is held on them, then tap on their mobile phone number.

Fig. 1.4 Contacts List.

If you are making a call to someone who is not on your contacts list:

- Tap the **Phone** app, shown here, then tap the 'Keypad' option at the bottom of the displayed 'Keypad' screen (shown in blue in Fig. 1.5), to display the keypad.

- Next, tap the recipient's phone number followed by the green phone screen-button to start the call (in Fig. 1.5, only the local code has been entered).

- If, on the other hand, the contacts option is selected at the bottom of the screen (to the left of the keypad option), the contacts list is displayed instead.

Fig. 1.5 Keypad Screen.

Receiving a Call

Two slightly different screens are displayed when receiving a call, depending on whether the phone is in 'Sleep' or 'Wake' mode.

If the iPhone is in 'Sleep' mode (you have pressed the 'Sleep/Wake' button which blanks the 'Home' screen and 'Locks' the phone), it displays the 'slide to answer' option, as shown in Fig. 1.6. Only the bottom half of the display is shown here – the name of the person calling is displayed at the top half.

Fig. 1.6 Slide in Direction of Arrow to Answer.

The white arrow in the displayed screen above, was added by me to show you the direction of 'slide' (from left to right).

When the phone is in use (not in sleep mode), you get the **Accept** and **Decline** options in the form of two screen buttons as shown in Fig. 1.7. This is because when the phone is in wake mode (being used or 'Unlocked), it is easier to answer with a tap on a button than using the slide finger move.

Fig. 1.7 The Button to Answer Display.

In both answering modes, two further buttons are displayed on the screen, namely **Remind Me** and **Messages**. Tapping the first, silences the ringing, and displays the options shown in Fig. 1.8 which are reminders to yourself to call back. Tapping either one of these two, disconnects the

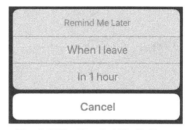

Fig. 1.8 The Remind Me Options.

call. The **Cancel** option, reverts the call to one of the two 'Answer' screens, as discussed earlier.

Tapping the **Messages** button, silences the ringing and displays a list of preselected messages, as shown in Fig. 1.9. which can be sent instantly to the caller. There is also an option to customise the text message to be sent, but this requires knowledge on how to use text messaging (more about this shortly). Tapping the **Cancel** option, reverts the call to one of the two answering modes described earlier.

Fig. 1.9 The Messages Options.

Using Text Messages

If you're not able to make a phone call, you can send a text. A text message will be delivered to the recipient immediately, provided they are in an area of good reception, otherwise it will be delivered the moment they move to such an area.

Sending a text message, saves time by not having to try over and over again to make a voice call to a person who might have either their phone switched off or are in an area of bad reception.

To send a text message, tap the **Messages** app, shown here (also refer to Fig. 1.1 on page 1). If you have already received messages from friends, the display might look similar to that in Fig. 1.10.

Tapping on any of the displayed messages, opens up the 'Chats' you have had with the particular person and allows you to respond to them, as shown in Fig. 1.11.

If you're starting a new text chat with someone, tap the 'New Message' icon at the top right in Fig. 1.10, also shown here. This opens a screen with a pulsating cursor adjacent to the 'To:' label and an on-screen keyboard.

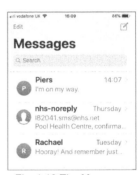

Fig. 1.10 The Messages Screen.

If the person you intend to send a text message to is in your **Contacts** list (how to create such a list will be discussed in Chapter 3), just type the beginning of their name and select them from the displayed list (use the option which includes their mobile number). If the person is not in your **Contacts** list, then just type their mobile number instead.

Fig. 1.11 The Chats Screen.

The actual message you want to send must be typed in the area at the bottom of the screen in Fig. 1.11.

It is a good idea to practice by sending a text message to yourself. For example, such a message might look similar to the one in Fig. 1.12.

There are several things to note in this text message screen. For a start, the message I typed and sent to my iPhone, displays in a blue background (after sending it). If this message was sent to a mobile other than an iPhone, it would display in a green background.

Below the sent message there is information on when the message was read by the recipient. Normally, you will get information on when the message was delivered, followed by

Fig. 1.12 A Message to Myself.

when it was read (more about this later). Below that, and in grey background, is what you receive back from the recipient which is the same message in this case, as I sent it to myself. So, in reality, what you send appears in a blue or green background and the answer you get back from the other person appears in a grey background.

If someone has sent you a text message, a number will appear at the top-right corner of the **Messages** app, signifying the number of messages received but not read, as shown here.

There is a lot more you can do with a text message, such as attaching a picture (by tapping the 'Camera' icon to the left of the area where you type your message) which allows you to take a picture there and then or use a picture in your **Photos** app) or, indeed, include a voice attachment by tapping and holding down the 'Microphone' or 'Voice indicator' icon to the right of the message entry area while you talk.

New facilities have been added with iOS12 and iOS13 (Apple's Operating System). For iOS12, tapping the 'Apple Store' icon (to the right of the 'Camera'), displays these, as shown in Fig.1.13 overleaf. For iOS13, they are already open.

These facilities appear as icons between the message insertion area and the on-screen keyboard. You can use any of these to select and attach to a message.

From left to right the icons allow you to access your 'Photos', the 'App Store', a series of 'Images', a 'Drawing' facility, your stored 'Music', 'eBay', 'Google Maps' and more besides by scrolling to the left.

The icons that appear on your phone, depend on the version of iPhone you have as well as the version of iOS, so don't get upset if in your case, you don't get all the facilities mentioned above.

Fig. 1.13 The Apple Store App Facilities.

Discussing these facilities in detail, is beyond the scope of this book, so I leave it to you to explore some of these later, after you have become more familiar with the iPhone.

Locking and Turning off the iPhone

To lock the iPhone immediately, just press the 'Sleep/Wake' button which blanks the screen. To unlock it, press the 'Sleep/Wake button again or press the 'Home' button. Both actions unlock the iPhone, though for versions prior to 6, you might have to drag the slider to the right to do so.

To turn off the iPhone, press and hold the 'Sleep/Wake' button until the 'Power off' slider' appears (Fig. 1.14). Drag the slider with your finger from left to right to turn the iPhone completely off. To turn it back on again (reboot), press and hold the 'Sleep/Wake' button until the Apple logo displays and eventually the 'Home' screen.

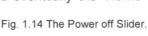

Fig. 1.14 The Power off Slider.

2

Using the E-Mail App

You can use the built-in **Mail** app of the iPhone to send and receive e-mail messages, but you must first configure it. You can use either Web-based or an IMAP-based (Internet Message Access Protocol) mail.

E-mail Configuration on the iPhone

When you first tap on the **Mail** app on the iPhone shown here (also refer to Fig. 1.1 on page 1), it displays the screen in Fig. 2.1 below.

As you can see, there are several Web-based e-mail clients, such as 'Google' mail or 'Outlook', and using any of these is easy and straightforward. What you need though, is your account details. I'll discuss one of these shortly.

If, however, your e-mail account is not a Web-based one, then you should tap the 'Other' option at the bottom of the list. This displays a series of screens that allow you to insert the details for industry-standard 'IMAP' e-mail accounts, to be discussed shortly.

Fig. 2.1 E-mail Configuration.

Configuring a Web-based E-mail Account

To configure, say, a 'Google' e-mail account which most people tend to use, tap the 'Google' entry on the list above to display the screen shown in Fig. 2.2 on the next page.

This is the first of a series of screens in which you are asked to:

- Type in your name, as shown here, then tap 'Next'.

- Enter your date of birth and your gender.

- Choose an e-mail address from a suggested list or create your own.

- Create a strong password of at least 8 characters with a mixture of letters (upper and lower case), numbers and symbols.

Fig. 2.2 Configuring a Google Account.

- Supply your phone number which will be used, amongst other options, to reset your password should you forget it.

- Agree to Google's terms of service and their right to process the information you've supplied.

Once all this information has been given and terms accepted, your account and e-mail address are created. Try it for yourself.

Configuring a Non-Web E-mail Account

Some people have more than one e-mail address, primarily for keeping private mail separate from work mail. So, if this is the case with you and, say, the second account is either with TalkTalk, BT or indeed any other non-Web mail account provider, then tap the 'Other' option in Fig. 2.1 on the previous page to display the screen in Fig. 2.4 shown on the next page.

If you have already configured a Web-based e-mail account, however, you can return to Fig. 2.1 by tapping the built-in **Settings** app, shown here, to display the screen in Fig. 2.3 below.

Scrolling down and tapping the 'Passwords & Accounts' entry, opens the screen shown in Fig. 2.4 below and tapping 'Add Mail Account' opens the screen in Fig. 2.1, but only if you have previously configured an e-mail account. Then tapping the 'Other' entry, opens the same screen as that in Fig. 2.4 so you can edit a previously configured account or add a new account.

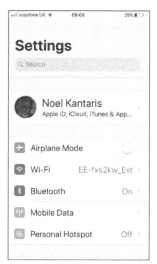

Fig. 2.3 The Settings Screen.

Fig. 2.4 Adding an Other-type Mail Account.

To add a further account, tap 'Add Mail Account' entry, in Fig. 2.4, to open a further screen shown in Fig. 2.5.

Fig. 2.5 E-mail Configuration.

Use the on-screen keyboard to type the required information. Until you finish providing all the information required, the 'Next' button at the top-right of Fig. 2.5 on the previous page, remains grey (inactive), but after entering everything you are asked to, the button becomes active and turns blue.

Tapping the blue 'Next' button, displays another screen, as shown in Fig. 2.6. Suggestions of what is expected in each field are displayed in light grey, as in Fig. 2.5 on the previous page, but are replaced the moment you start typing. The 'Host Name' within the fields of 'INCOMING' and 'OUTGOING' mail servers are specific to your e-mail provider.

Finally, tapping the 'Next' button on the screen in Fig. 2.6 display the last configuration screen, as shown in Fig. 2.7. 'IMAP' stands for Internet Message Access Protocol and is a method of accessing and storing mail on your provider's mail server.

Fig. 2.6 New E-mail Configuration.

Fig. 2.7 The IMAP Screen.

Tapping the 'Save' button, saves the newly created account and allows you to receive and send e-mail messages. The best way of testing such an account is by sending a test e-mail to yourself and see if you receive it back.

E-mail Folders

Having configured your e-mail account or accounts as discussed previously, when you now tap the **Mail** app, you are presented with a screen of your 'Mailbox' or 'Mailboxes' (if you have configured more than one e-mail address). In my case, the display is as shown in Fig. 2.8 on the next page.

Note that here, I have two 'Mailboxes', one which is a non-Web based and a second one which is with Gmail.

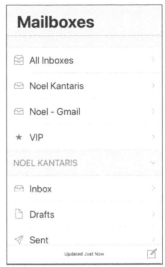

Fig. 2.8 Mailboxes Screen.

Tapping the 'All Inboxes' entry, displays all the e-mail messages sent to me in both accounts, as shown in Fig. 2.9 below.

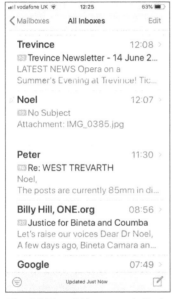

Fig. 2.9 E-mail Messages in Both Accounts.

Tapping the 'Mailboxes' entry at the top-left of the screen in Fig. 2.9, takes you back to the screen in Fig. 2.8 (the arrowhead pointing to the left, indicates that you will be sent to the previous screen).

Next, tapping the 'Gmail' account entry in the top-half of Fig. 2.8, displays all the e-mail messages sent to that account. In the bottom-half of the screen in Fig. 2.8, there is a list of all the e-mail folders under the highlighted account, such as 'Inbox', 'Drafts', 'Sent' and a lot more besides, which can be displayed by scrolling down the screen.

Each account has their separate e-mail folders, including folders for 'Junk' messages and 'Trash' in which all the messages you delete go.

Unsolicited e-mail messages normally end up in the 'Junk' folder, especially misspelled ones or messages trying to sell you something. You should occasionally check the 'Junk' folder, to see if a genuine e-mail has gone there by mistake.

Writing and Sending an E-mail

Just as discussed in the previous chapter on page 6, starting a new e-mail is similar to starting a new message. Tap the 'New' e-mail icon shown at the bottom-right of Fig. 2.9, also shown here, to open the screen in Fig. 2.10 below.

If the person you intend to send an e-mail to is in your **Contacts** list (see next Chapter on how to create such a list), just type, where the cursor is pulsating to the right of the 'To:' box, the beginning of their name and select them from the displayed list (the option which includes their e-mail address). If the person is not in your **Contacts** list, then just type in their e-mail address. Once an address is inserted, the 'Send' button becomes active.

From iOS12.3 and later, the 'Cc' and 'Bcc' boxes appear on the same line, but tapping on this line, separates the boxes. In earlier versions of the iOS, the 'Cc/Bcc' and 'From' boxes display on separate lines, while tapping on 'Cc/Bcc' line

Fig. 2.10 Starting a New E-mail.

separates them. In even earlier versions of the iOS, only the 'Cc' box displays, while the 'Bcc' box had to be activated separately using the **Settings** app, then the **Mail** option.

- 'Cc' (Carbon copy) is where you include the address of additional persons that you would like to receive the same message.

- 'Bcc' (Blind carbon copy) is where you include the address of a person you want to receive the same e-mail, but the other recipients are unaware of that fact.

- The sender's address is automatically inserted in the 'From' box.

Each e-mail should have a short subject, that will appear in the recipient's 'Inbox' when the e-mail is received.

The main body of the e-mail is typed below the subject line once you tap at that spot and the pulsating cursor appears there. Try sending a short text message to yourself with an appropriate subject line, then switch to your 'Inbox' to see how it appears.

Editing Text on the iPhone

The iPhone's keyboard does not have any cursor keys, so to correct any mistakes, tap the 'Backspace key, shown here, to move from your current position to the left one character with each tap of the key.

This might be convenient if you just made the mistake, but not good enough if you finish typing a page and then spotted a mistake somewhere in the middle of a paragraph. To see how you can edit such text, type a new e-mail, one that is at least a few lines long and deliberately introduce a misspelled word in the middle of it, then try to edit it before sending it.

For an iPhone with the new Operating System (iOS13), touch the insertion pointer and drag it to the right of the character or word you want to edit, then use the 'Backspace' key to delete the unwanted characters. For iPhones with an iOS prior to iOS13, tap near the word you want to edit and once the insertion pointer is pulsating, press your finger on the screen and when the magnifying glass appears, move your finger to the right of the character or word you want to edit, as shown in Fig. 2.11 on the next page.

Directions

Whisk egg whites for 90 seconds.   ght in the bo
Add granulated sugar & whisk for a fu{ace in an ai{s.
Switch off & fold in the caster sugar.
Spoon onto a baking tray & bake overni   ottom oven of the Aga.
Cool on a wire tray. As soon as cool, place in an airtight container.

Fig. 2.11 Moving the Insertion Pointer.

Once the insertion line in the middle of the magnifying glass is in the correct position, lift your finger from the screen and use the 'Backspace' key to remove the mistake, then type the replacement character of word.

To copy or enhance a word or a section of text for all iPhones using any iOS, touch the iPhone's screen on the first word of the text to display what is shown in Fig. 2.12. Here, I have turned the iPhone on its side in a way so that the 'Home' button is on your right. This allows more choices to be displayed on the 'Options' bar, as shown below.

Fig. 2.12 Selecting a Word.

Tapping on the word 'Select' in the 'Options' bar, puts handles around the word as shown in Fig. 2.13 on the next page.

Tapping the right-arrowhead displays the available enhancements for the selected text as shown in Fig. 2.13.

Fig. 2.13 Commands and Enhancements for Selected Word.

If you want to increase the selection, touch one of the handles and either drag the top one up or the bottom one down. An example of this is shown in Fig. 2.14 below.

Fig. 2.14 Selecting a Section of Text.

You can now 'Cut' (remove) or 'Copy' the marked selection of text and move it to another part of the text by moving the insertion pointer where you want to insert the text, then use the 'Paste' option to insert it there. The 'Paste' option will only appear on the bar once you have copied text.

I suggest you use your own example so that you can practice the editing techniques discussed above. The more you practice the easier it becomes.

Other Keyboard Layouts

The default keyboard is 'alphabetic'. For a predominately 'numeric' keyboard tap the '123' key shown upper left. A 'symbol' keyboard can be reached from within the 'numeric' one by tapping the 'symbol' key shown on the right. To return to the 'alphabetic' keyboard tap the 'ABC' key shown lower left.

Deleting E-mail Messages

You can delete an e-mail message by selecting it and tapping the 'Bin' icon at the bottom of the screen, as shown in Fig. 2.15 below.

However, all that this action does is to place unwanted e-mails in the 'Trash' folder (renamed 'Bin' in iOS13). The icons from left to right at the bottom of Fig. 2.15, for pre-iOS13, allow you to:

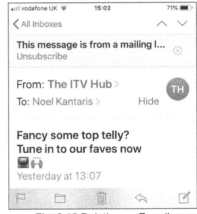

Fig. 2.15 Deleting an E-mail.

- Flag, Mark as Unread, Move to Junk and Notify Me.

- Move e-mails to another (displayed) folder.

- Delete the e-mail displayed.

- Reply, Forward and Print e-mail messages.

If you delete a message by mistake, navigate back to your 'Mailbox' or 'Mailboxes' select the appropriate 'Trash' (or 'Bin' in iOS13) folder, find the deleted e-mail, tap it to select it, then for pre-iOS13 tap on the second icon from the left and choose the 'Inbox' folder from the displayed list of folders to restore the deleted e-mail. In iOS13, tap the curved arrowhead at the bottom-left of the screen to display options to 'Reply', 'Forward', 'Flag', 'Move', 'Archive', etc.

In pre-iOS13, every e-mail held in the 'Trash' folder can be deleted by tapping the folder to display its contents, then tapping the 'Edit' button, followed by the 'Delete All' button at the bottom-right of the screen. In the case of iOS13 tap the 'Bin' folder, then the 'Select All' option, followed by 'Delete'.

Adding Another Language Keyboard

From iPhone 5 and later models, adding another language keyboard and flicking from one language to the other, has been made very easy.

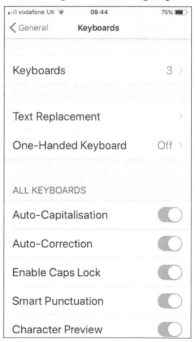

To add another language keyboard, go to **Settings**, 'General' and select 'Keyboard' to display the screen in Fig. 2.16.

From this screen you can add or remove various options relating to your keyboard. Tapping on the 'Keyboards' option near the top of the screen, displays the keyboards now being used on your iPhone. In my case three keyboards are being used, as indicated in Fig. 2.16.

Fig. 2.16 The Keyboards Screen.

To add another language keyboard, tap on 'Add New Keyboard' option to first display a variety of English keyboards, as shown in Fig. 2.17, before reaching other types of keyboards.

As an example, I have added a French keyboard. Unwanted keyboards can be deleted by tapping the 'Keyboards' option in Fig. 2.16 on the previous page, to reveal all the keyboards being used.

Next tap 'Edit' at the top-right of the displayed screen, then tap the negative red sign that appears against the keyboard you want to remove and finally tap the red 'Delete' button.

Fig. 2.17 The Add New Keyboard Screen.

Fig. 2.18 Deleting a Keyboard.

Each time you tap the 'Globe' the keyboard rotates through the chosen keyboards, including the 'Emoji' keyboard – a collection of little images (smiling or sad faces, hearts, etc.), that you can include in you messages.

To use a different keyboard to the default while you are typing, click the 'Globe' next to the '123' key, shown in Fig. 2.19.

Fig. 2.19 Switching Keyboards.

3

Contacts & Calendar

This chapter covers the **Contacts** app which should be used with both text messaging (you will need to include a mobile number) and e-mail messaging (you will need to include an e-mail address), and the **Calendar** app which is your personal assistant and can be used to remind you of birthdays, appointment, including scheduled holidays.

The Contacts App

The **Contacts** app was introduced briefly earlier when discussing text messages in Chapter 1 (page 3). To have a closer look at this app, tap the **Contacts** icon on the 'Home' screen (see page 1), also shown here, to open all the contacts currently on your iPhone.

If your 'Contacts' list is empty, what is displayed is your name, as shown in Fig. 3.1. Note the + icon at the top-right of the screen which you tap to add a new contact.

On the right edge of the same screen, you can see the whole alphabet and tapping on a given letter, takes you to the nearest entry beginning with that letter. This, of course is, only useful if you have created a sizeable number of contacts.

Fig. 3.1 My Card Screen.

Tapping the entry at the top of the screen in Fig. 3.1, displays the information held on you, which includes your mobile telephone number (the iPhone already knows it), as shown in Fig. 3.2 below.

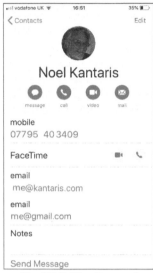

To add an e-mail address, tap the 'Edit' icon at the top-right of the screen, then tap to move the cursor within a required field and use the on-screen keyboard that displays to type any additional information. When you finish editing, tap the 'Done' icon that replaces the 'Edit' icon, to save the changes made.

To add another person in your **Contacts** list, tap the 'Contacts' icon at the top-left of the above screen, to return to the screen in Fig. 3.1 on the previous page, then tap on the $+$ icon to open the screen in Fig. 3.3.

Fig. 3.2 Editing Personal Information.

In the 'New Contact' screen, I typed 'John' in the 'First name' field. You could then add a surname in the 'Last name' field, in which case your contacts will display by default, surname first followed by first name. If you know, their mobile number and e-mail address, type them in the appropriate fields, then tap 'Done' to save the new contact.

There are other ways of creating new contacts, as we shall see next.

Fig. 3.3 Adding a New Contact.

Adding a New Contact from a Received E-mail

If someone who is not in your **Contacts** sends you an e-mail and you want to include this person on your list of contacts, do the following:

- Tap on the e-mail to open it, part of which is shown in Fig. 3.4.

- Tap on 'Details' at top-right of the screen, then touch and hold the sender's name to highlight it, as shown in Fig. 3.5.

- Lifting your finger off the screen, opens the screen displayed in Fig. 3.6.

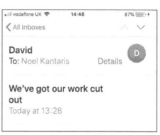

Fig. 3.4 Sender's E-mail.

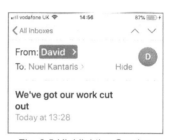

Fig. 3.5 Highlighting Sender.

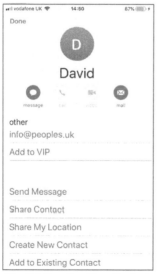

Fig. 3.6 Creating New Contact.

From the displayed list of options, choose 'Create New Contact' or, if you prefer, one of the other options.

If you tap 'Done' at the top-left of the screen, you will be taken back to the screen in Fig. 3.4.

Adding a New Contact from a Received Text

If someone who is not in your **Contacts** sends you a text message and you want to include this person on your list of contacts, do the following:

- Tap the text message to open it. This might look something similar to Fig. 3.7.

- Tap on the sender's photo area to display Fig. 3.8. I only show here the top of the screen.

- Tap the third option labelled 'Info' to display the screen in Fig. 3.9.

- Next, tap the faint right-arrowhead, which I've marked with a grey circle so you can locate it easily on your screen, to open the screen in Fig. 3.10.

- To create a new contact, simply tap the second option.

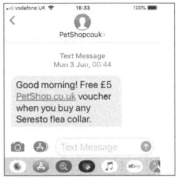

Fig. 3.7 Sender's Text Message.

Fig. 3.8 Additional Options.

Fig. 3.9 Sender's Details.

If you tap 'Done' in Fig. 3.9, you will be taken back to the screen of Fig. 3.8.

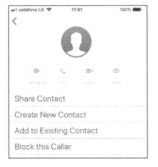

Fig. 3.10 Creating a New Contact.

In some of the screens displayed on the iPhone, you would have noticed the blue arrowheads '<' and '>' which you tap to take you to the previous or next screen, respectively.

Changing the Contacts Displayed Order

If you are like me, you might prefer to have your contacts displayed with their first name first, followed by their surname. It makes it easier to find a certain female friend by their first name rather than by their surname, particularly if they got married and changed their surname.

To do this, tap the all important **Settings** app on the 'Home' screen, also shown here, then scroll down to 'Contacts' and tap the entry to display the screen in Fig. 3.11. Only the top part of the screen is shown here.

Next tap in turn on 'Sort Order' then 'Display Order' and change each from the default setting shown in Fig. 3.11 to 'First, Last' on the secondary screens that open. It is as simple as that. Of course, if you don't like this display order, you can easily revert to the default.

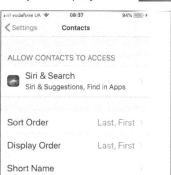

Fig. 3.11 Changing Display Order.

Deleting a Redundant Contact

To remove a person from your contacts list, simply tap on their name to display the information held on them, then tap the 'Edit' icon at the top-right of the screen, then scroll to the very bottom of the screen and tap the 'Delete Contact' option, shown in Fig. 3.12.

Fig. 3.12 Deleting a Contact.

The Calendar App

As I've said earlier, without the **Calendar** app to remind me what I have to do next, I'll be lost, so in what follows I'll show you how to use it to help you never to forger a meeting, an appointment, a birthday or when to de-flea your cat or dog!

Tapping on the **Calendar** app shown here (see also the 'Home' screen in Fig. 1.1 on page 1, where it appears within a folder called **Time&Calen** - tap the folder to display the **Clock** and **Calendar** apps magnified, then tap the latter), to open the screen in Fig. 3.13. Folders will be discussed in Chapter 5.

If, however, a different screen is displayed, tap today's date highlighted in red in every screen, then the < (red arrowhead) at the top left of the screen to display the yearly view as in Fig. 3.13.

Fig. 3.13 Calendar's Yearly View.

Fig. 3.14 Calendar's Monthly View.

To see more detail, tap on today's date on the yearly view, marked in red, to display a monthly view, as shown in Fig. 3.14.

The grey dots that appear under dates in the monthly view of **Calendar** (Fig. 3.14 on the previous page), signify pre-existing entries. Tapping on such an entry, displays a screen with that entry's details. If you haven't created any entries yet, such dots will not be present.

Creating a Calendar Event

To create a **Calendar** event, tap the red plus icon at the top-right of either the yearly of monthly views, also shown +
here, to display the screen in Fig. 3.15 below.

In the 'Title' field, I have already typed an event's name. Tapping on the date given in the 'Starts' field, displays below it a scrolling date and time entries for you to choose from – scroll the date first to the required date, then do the same with the time.

Next, scroll down to the 'Repeat' field and select an appropriate repeat period.

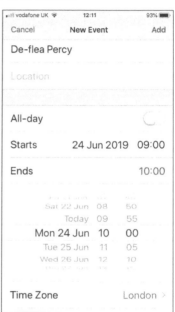

Fig. 3.15 Creating a New Event.

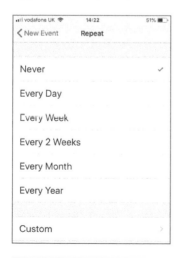

For a birthday the repeat period will be 'Every Year', while for an appointment it might be 'Never', but to keep Percy free of fleas, it has to be every 28 days.

Fig. 3.16 Creating a Repeat Period.

To achieve a 28 day alert period, select 'Custom' and in the next screen tap the 'Every' day field and select 28 from the rolling clock, then tap the 'Repeat' icon at the top left of the screen to return to the previous screen, then tap the 'New Event' icon at the top left of the screen, then scroll to the bottom of the 'New Entry' screen and tap the 'Alert' field to display a screen similar to that in Fig. 3.17.

Selecting '1 hour before' is quite adequate in this case, though for a birthday you might want to choose '2 days before' to give you time to buy a card and post it. However, if the card is to be posted abroad, a '1 week before' might be better.

Finally, tap the 'Add' icon at the top right of the 'New Event' screen to save your creation.

Fig. 3.17 Creating an Alert.

Next, tap the < icon at the top left of the screen to return to the monthly view. Tapping the icon at the top of the monthly view, also shown here, ⌐ displays the current month only. Tapping it again, returns you to the monthly view.

If you now tap on the current date, a list of current entries (only one in this case) is displayed, as shown in Fig. 3.18.

Note that the screen opens near the actual 'current time', so you might have to scroll up or down to see the current event.

Fig. 3.18 Displaying a Current Event.

Editing a Calendar Entry

To edit an event, tap on it, to display a screen similar to that of Fig. 3.19. Here, you have the choice to either 'Delete' the event or edit it. To do the latter, tap the 'Edit' icon at the top right of the screen to open the screen in Fig. 3.20.

Fig. 3.19 Displaying an Event.

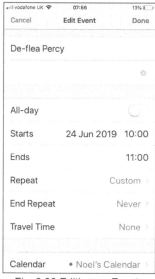

Fig. 3.20 Editing an Event.

Fig. 3.21 Displaying a Current

Having edited the displayed repeat event, tap the 'Done' icon at the top right of the screen. You'll be asked to choose between 'Save for this event only' or 'Save for future events', as shown in Fig. 3.21.

Naturally, if the event is a repeat event, and you want to change this and all future events, you should choose the latter, but if you want the changes to affect this event only, but leave all future occurrences unchanged, then select the 'Save for this event only' option. After selecting an option, the screen reverts to that of Fig. 3.19.

Now, if you tap the < icon at the top left in Fig. 3.19 on the previous page (I did not include the date that appears after the icon, as this might be different for you - it depends when you actually carried out the editing of the selected event), the screen changes to that shown in Fig. 3.22.

Again, in your case this screen will look different, as it is dependant on the events you have stored in the **Calendar**.

Note the 'three line' icon at the top of Fig. 3.22, also shown here. When you tap this icon, it displays the last accessed event and opens it in a 'Daily' view, as shown earlier in Fig. 3.18 (page 26). Tapping it again reverts the screen to that of Fig. 3.22.

Finally, note the icon 'Calendars' at the bottom of the screen in Fig. 3.22. Tapping it, displays all the 'Calendars' you have configured on your phone, as shown in Fig. 3.23 for my iPhone.

Fig. 3.22 Displaying all Events.

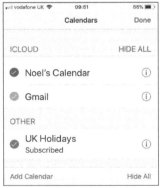

Fig. 3.23 Showing all Configured Calendars.

It is possible to subscribe to additional 'Calendars', such as one that displays exclusively 'UK School Holidays', or one that lists specific schedules of any club or society, but you might have to pay for the service. The possibilities are endless, so I leave it to you to explore when the need arises. There are lots of Websites on the Internet that specialise for such needs.

4

Safari Browser & iCloud

The 'Safari' browser allows you to display Websites on the Internet, while the 'iCloud' facility manages your 'Contacts', 'Calendar' and a lot more, including a 'Backup' facility.

The Safari Browser App

By default, the 'Safari' icon, shown here, is found on the 'Dock' area of the iPhone's screen, which makes it accessible from all the 'Home' screens, not just the first one. Tapping it, opens the app, as shown in Fig. 4.1, waiting for you to type a search criteria using the on-screen keyboard.

If you type 'Dogs rescue' on the 'Search bar', then tap the 'Go' icon at the bottom-right of

Fig. 4.1 The Safari Opening Screen.

the screen, you'll get a result similar to that in Fig. 4.2.

Fig. 4.2 Search Results.

The first thing to notice here is that 'Google' has found some results after asking if it could use your location so that it could find results nearby.

To see why 'Google' is used here, go to 'Settings', scroll down and tap on 'Safari' which opens a screen with an option to select a 'Search Engine'. Tap on this to display available search engines, as shown in Fig. 4.3. Choose whichever search engine you prefer by tapping it. A tick appears to the right of the chosen one.

Fig. 4.3 Search Engine Selection.

It is important to understand the difference between a 'Browser' and a 'Search Engine', so what follows is a simple definition for both:

- A 'Browser' such as 'Safari', 'Edge', 'Google Chrome' and others is used to access various Websites and Web pages.

- A 'Search Engine' such as 'Google', 'Bing', 'Yahoo' and others is used to search for a particular document on the Internet when specific keywords are entered.

So, in Fig. 4.3 above, **Safari** is used to display the results found by **Google**.

Tabs in Safari and Private Browsing

Now return to **Safari**'s display shown in Fig. 4.2 on the previous page (if you have lost that Web page, carry out a new search), then tap the 'tabs' icon at the bottom of the screen, also shown here, then tap the 'plus' icon that appears at the bottom of the screen, also shown here.

Next, type 'Dog's food' as the new search criteria on the **Safari** screen and tap the 'Go' icon at the bottom-right of the screen to reveal several new Websites. Select the 'Tailor-made Dog Food' entry.

In addition, you'll also have to look after the poor animal, so tap the 'tabs' icon again, then tap the 'plus' icon and search for 'Dog vets near me'. Finally, tap the 'tabs' icon again to obtain a screen similar to that shown in Fig. 4.4.

Fig. 4.4 Safari Tabs.

What is displayed here is the result of three searches in tab view. It is easy to view any of them by just tapping on it.

Tabs were introduced by Apple with iOS6, which means that it is available to all iPhones from version 4S to the latest ones.

You can easily delete any tab by simply tapping on the 'X' icon at the top left of each. If, however you have lots of tabs open, then an easier way is to tap the 'Done' icon at the bottom of Fig. 4.4 to reveal the 'tabs' icon, then place your finger on it and hold it there for a second, until the screen in Fig. 4.5 is displayed.

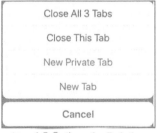

Fig. 4.5 Options for Deleting Tabs in Safari.

Use any of these options to either close a selected tab or all the opened tabs. You could even open a 'New Tab' or a 'New Private Tab'.

Private Browsing, introduced first with iOS5, blocks Websites from placing cookies (very small code) on your iPhone which are used to track and collect data, such as which Websites you visit, so that personalised adverts can be sent to you.

However, cookies can also enable sites to remember users and help them to automatically sign-in when revisiting such sites. So **Private Browsing** can have both positive and negative effects, depending on your view on security.

Toolbars in Safari

While using **Safari** to browse Websites on the Internet, various toolbars display at the top and bottom of the **Safari** screen. These have various icons which when tapped have the following effect:

    ⟳   Refreshes the current Web page (displays at top).

    < >   Navigates backward and forward within an open Web site (displays at bottom).

    📖   Opens your **Bookmarks** including **Favourites**, **Reading List** and **History** (all displaying at the top).

    ⬆   **Sends** or **Copies** the current Web page to various destinations as shown in Fig. 4.6 (displays at bottom).

Fig. 4.6 Web Page Destinations.

You can swipe to the left to see additional destinations.

For example, a current Web page can be sent as an attachment to a friend using 'Messages' or in an 'e-mail'. It can also be copied, sent to a printer, added to a reading list or added to a bookmark. The list of what you can do and which method you employ is almost endless.

On the tab area of the screen, as we have already seen, there are three further icons which when tapped allow you to:

    +   Open additional tabs (browser windows).

    ×   Close the active tab.

    Private   Browse the Internet privately.

Tabs can be rearranged on the screen by pressing on them lightly and dragging them up or down.

Adding Safari Bookmarks

To add a bookmark, visit the Website in **Safari**, then tap the 'Send' icon to open the screen shown in Fig. 4.6 on the previous page. Next, using the **Add Bookmark** option (in

iOS13 you'll have to scroll down), places the bookmark at the end of the existing list, if there is one there. You can even use the **Add to Favourites** or the **Add to Home Screen** option to place, in the latter case, a shortcut icon to it on the 'Home' screen.

As an example of using the last option mentioned above, search the Internet for Wikipedia. 'Today's featured article' displays as a Web page, then tap the 'Send' icon and select the **Add to Home Screen** option from the displayed screen. This places the 'Wikepedia' icon on the 'Home' page so as to be easily accessible to you. Finally, you are allowed to type an

appropriate name and tap the 'Done' icon at the bottom-right of the screen to place the icon shown here, on the 'Home' screen.

Deleting Safari Bookmarks

You can delete unwanted bookmarks by using two different methods:

- To use the first method, tap the 'Edit' icon at the bottom-right of the screen in Fig. 4.7 to display Fig. 4.8, then tap the icon shown here, to display the red 'Delete' icon. Tap this to delete the bookmark.

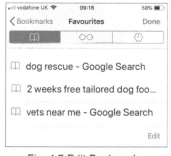

Fig. 4.7 Edit Bookmarks.

Fig. 4.8 Delete a Bookmark.

- To use the second method, first touch the bookmark
to be deleted, then slide
your finger to the left to
display the red 'Delete'
icon shown in Fig. 4.9.
Tap this to delete the
bookmark.

In both cases, tapping the blue
'Done' icon at the bottom-right of
the screen, returns you to the list
of Fig. 4.7 on the previous page.

Fig. 4.9 Delete a Bookmark.

Tapping **Reading List**, displays a list of all the articles you
stored in there for reading later, while tapping **History**,
displays a list of sites you have visited at specified dates.

iCloud and iCloud Drive

There is a difference between **iCloud** and **iCloud Drive**. The
former is basically a storage space, while the latter is a
cloud-based facility for sharing data between iOS devices.

The iCloud Service

How to check that 'iCloud' is turned on, depends on the
version of iOS on your iPhone:

- For iOS later than 10.2,
go to **Settings**, tap on the
'Apple profile' at the top of
the 'Settings menu' as
shown here for my iPhone
in Fig. 4.10, then tap on
the 'iCloud' entry that is
displayed on the 'Apple
ID' screen shown in
Fig. 4.11 on the next
page.

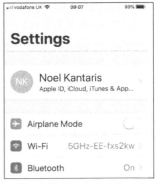

Fig. 4.10 Checking iCloud.

- For versions of iOS10.2 or earlier, you'll find 'iCloud' in **Settings**, immediately below the 'Control Centre' entry which opens a similar screen to Fig. 4.11.

- Next, tap the 'iCloud' entry to see how much storage you have and make sure that 'Photos', 'Contacts', 'Calendars', and 'Reminders' are switched on, as shown in Fig. 4.12.

Fig. 4.11 The App ID Screen.

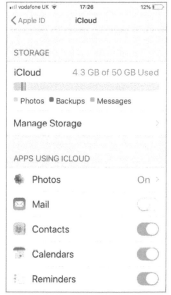

Fig. 4.12 Edit Bookmarks.

You are provided with a free 5 GB of storage capacity (in my case, I pay a small fee to get 50 GB, as shown in Fig. 4.12).

The 'iCloud' service acts as a kind of depositary for your data mainly for automatic backups of your phone. Such backups will also include all purchases you have made from Apple stores. For example, it stores all music or TV shows you bought from 'iTunes', books from 'iBookstore', apps from the 'App Store', but does not include other similar items purchased from non-Apple outlets.

Forcing a Backup

Sometimes it might be necessary to force a backup there and then, say because you made some major changes and you want to make sure to back them up. To do this, scroll down from the display of Fig. 4.12 on the previous page to display what appears in Fig. 4.13.

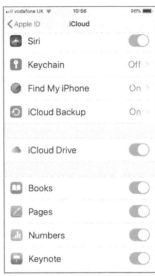

Next, tap on 'iCloud Backup' to open a further screen in which you can select the option to 'Back Up Now'. It only takes half a minute to complete such a backup.

While you are on the screen of Fig. 4.13, make sure that the options shown are turned on. This will facilitate exchange of data between your various Apple devices.

Fig. 4.13 The App ID Screen.

The iCloud Drive

The 'iCloud Drive' is part of 'iCloud'. While 'iCloud' serves to backup your device and sync limited kinds of data to other Apple devices, 'iCloud Drive' shares data stored in it with other devices. For example, documents, photos, contacts and calendars, etc., is pushed to other iOS devices and computers set up with the same account.

The difference between 'iCloud Drive' and other similar services like 'Dropbox' and 'Google Drive' is that instead of accessing your data via the 'iCloud Drive' app directly, you do so via different apps capable of accessing such data. For example, you access your photos in 'iCloud Drive' via the 'Photos' app, your contacts via the 'Contacts' app, your calendars via the 'Calendars' app, your books via the 'Books' app, your documents via apps that support such capability, like 'Word', 'Excel', 'Power Point', etc.

The iCloud Service on a Windows PC

On PCs this service is available on Windows 7 through to Windows 10. Just as well, because all your 'Contacts' and 'Calendars' might be on a PC, and it would be unthinkable to have to type all this information into the iPhone!

To access iCloud's services on a PC, start 'Microsoft Edge' (or a browser of your preference, if supported) and first set its zoom level to 100% in the **View**, **Zoom** menu option. Then type in the address bar

www.icloud.com

which opens the screen shown in Fig. 4.14 below.

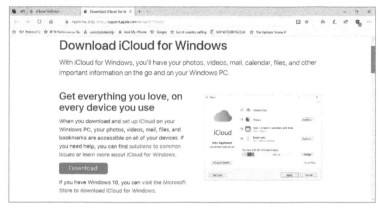

Fig. 4.14 The Download iCloud Screen on a Windows PC.

Click the 'Download' button which will ask you whether you want to 'Run' or 'Save' the program. Selecting to 'Run', starts the download process which takes just over half an hour to complete. Restarting your PC, completes the configuration and places the 'iCloud' icon on the desktop, shown here and places an 'iCloud Control Panel' icon (but named 'iCloud') on the PC's 'Taskbar'.

Double-clicking the desktop icon, displays the 'Sign in' Apple screen, shown in Fig. 4.15 on the next page, where you'll have to enter your Apple ID. Pressing the right-arrow button asks for your Password. Do check the square 'Keep me signed in', before you click the final right-arrow button.

Next, an 'Apple ID Verification Code' is sent to your iPhone, which you have to enter in the PC's screen to continue with the sign in procedure. If you don't check the little white square to keep you signed in, you'll have to repeat the whole of this procedure, including the 'ID Verification', every time you double-click the 'iCloud' icon on your PC's desktop.

Fig. 4.15 The Sign in to iCloud Screen on the PC.

Having completed the sign in to the 'iCloud' procedure correctly, the screen in Fig. 4.16 is displayed.

Fig. 4.16 The iCloud Screen on a Windows PC.

Now your PC is capable of getting its data from the 'iCloud' like all your other iOS devices, like iPhone, iPad, etc.

Next, click the 'iCloud Control Panel' icon on the 'Taskbar' bar to open the screen shown in Fig. 4.17 on the next page.

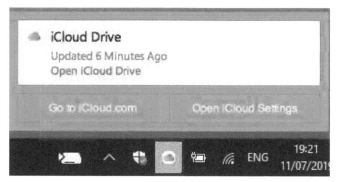

Fig. 4.17 The iCloud Control Panel on a Windows 10 PC.

If you were to click the 'Go to iCloud.com' button, the screen in Fig. 4.16 would display, but clicking on the 'Open iCloud Settings' button instead, displays the screen in Fig. 4.18.

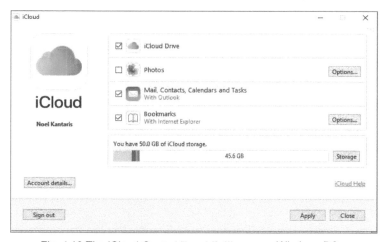

Fig. 4.18 The iCloud Control Panel Settings on a Windows PC.

Check everything you want to transfer from your PC to the 'iCloud', except 'Photos'. It is unwise to transfer all your photos from your PC to the 'iCloud', as you might exceed the 5 GB of free space allocated to you. There is a better method of dealing selectively with photos which will be discussed in Chapter 6. **Be warned**: Clicking the 'Apply' button, synchs all the checked data to 'iCloud'.

If you now return to the screen in Fig. 4.16 (if you don't have it open on your PC, double-click the 'iCloud' icon on your desktop), you'll find that every app on it gets its data from the 'iCloud'. All your 'Contacts', 'Calendar' appointments are there for you to access and add to or edit and any changes will be pushed to your other iOS devices.

There are two apps of interest on the 'iCloud' for pre-iOS13 devices; 'Find iPhone' and 'Find Friends', which need to be discussed in a little more detail. With iOS13 these two apps have been combined into one (see end of this chapter).

The iCloud Find iPhone App

To locate your iPhone, should you leave it on a train or have it stolen, you need to carry out the following procedure:

- Click the **Settings** app icon on the 'Home' screen, shown here, to open the 'Settings' screen shown in Fig. 4.19 below.

- Tap on your profile (your name at the very top of the screen). For iOS10.2 or earlier, tap the **Settings** icon, then scroll down to 'iCloud' and scroll to the bottom and tap 'Find My iPhone'. Next, turn on 'Find My iPhone' and 'Send Last Location'. If you are asked to sign in, enter your Apple ID and Password.

- Once all requirements are completed, the 'Find iPhone' app icon, shown here, is placed on your 'Home' screen.

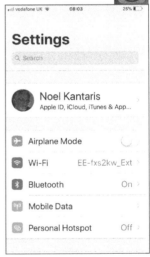

Fig. 4.19 The Settings Screen.

- Tapping the 'Find iPhone' icon displays all your Apple devices, as shown in Fig. 4.20 on the next page.

- In my case, there are two devices registered, an 'iPhone' and an 'iPad'. As an example, I used my 'iPhone' to locate my 'iPad'. You could also use the 'Find iPhone' app on your PC's 'iCloud' screen (see Fig. 4.16 on page 40).

- No matter from where you initiated the 'Find iPhone' app, you'll be asked to sign in with your Apple ID and Password. The device then displays on a map on your screen, as shown in Fig. 4.20. Here, my 'iPad' is on my desk, hence 0 miles away.

Fig. 4.20 The Find iPhone Screen.

- Tapping on the device you want to find, an additional screen is displayed with the option 'Actions' at the bottom of it. Tapping this option, displays the screen in Fig. 4.21.

Note the three options at the bottom of the screen in Fig. 4.21. You can now decide to:

(a) Send a sound to the lost device, in case you misplaced it within the house.

(b) Initiate a 'Lost Mode' which lets you lock and track the missing device and also provide contact information.

Fig. 4.21 The Actions Screen.

(c) 'Erase' the device's content, but an erased device cannot be located or tracked.

If you loose one of your Apple devices and you report it to the police, they will ask you for the device's serial number. This can be found in **Settings**, 'General', 'About'. Touching it on the screen, allows you to copy it.

Next, tap on the **Notes** app (see page 78), then the 'New Note' icon and paste the serial number in it. In this way, you can access **Notes** from your PC's 'iCloud' screen or any of your other Apple devices and find the serial numbers, if and when you are required to do so.

The iCloud Find Friends App

Of a lesser importance is the **Find Friends** app which allows you to locate your friends and family members from your iPhone, iPad or PC. The people you are trying to find must have an Apple device and they must be in your contacts list. Obviously you need to be

connected to the Internet and you must have an 'iCloud' account. Locating and tapping the app icon, displays Fig. 4.22.

Tapping the 'Add Friends' option, displays an e-mail screen in which you choose the name of the friend you would like to be friends with. The e-mail is then sent to that person who is informed of the request and is asked to either agree or disagree.

However, not many people are agreeable to be tracked, but if you have young or venerable children or someone who is going to a dangerous place, then the app might prove very useful indeed.

Fig. 4.22 The Find My Friends Screen.

The Combined 'Find My' App in iOS13

When you first start this app, shown here, you are asked permission to 'access your location'. Having given your permission, a screen similar to that in Fig. 4.23 is displayed.

Next, scroll to the bottom of the screen and tap 'Continue' to display Fig. 4.24.

Welcome to Find My

Two Apps Became One
Find My Friends and Find My iPhone are now combined in a single app.

Location Updates
Stay in touch with the people you care about by receiving notifications about their location.

Offline Finding
Improve the chance of finding your devices even when they're not connected to the internet.

Fig. 4.23 The Combined 'Find My' App Initial Screen.

Fig. 4.24 The Combined 'Find My' App screen.

At the bottom of the screen in Fig. 4.24, you see 3 icons:

The first icon is labelled 'People' depicting the name of a person that has agreed to be tracked with their whereabouts shown on a map.

The second icon Is labelled 'Devices' and when tapped displays all your devices for you to choose which one you want to trace.

The third icon is labelled 'Me' and when tapped displays your current location (that of your iPhone).

5

Apps, Screens & Passcodes

In this chapter, I first discuss how to organise apps on the 'Home' screen and how to close or delete running apps, before showing you how to customise your iPhone's screen. Next, I discuss your iPhone's data security by introducing passcodes and finally I show you how to search for topics using Siri, the iPhone's speaking assistant.

Multitasking with Apps on the iPhone

As discussed earlier, you can open any number of apps by simply tapping their icon on the 'Home' screen of your iPhone. As you open one app after another, all opened apps are kept running so that you can switch easily from one to the other. To see running apps, double-click the 'Home' button to display a screen similar to that in Fig. 5.1. Here, only three running apps are visible, even though there are several others running.

To select a different running app, simply place your finger on the screen, then slowly move your finger from left to right (you can also do the reverse movement if you go past the one you are looking for), to reveal the app you want, then tap on it to open it in full screen.

Fig. 5.1 Running Apps on an iPhone.

Closing Running Apps

Running apps consume battery power, so it is wise to close them often. You can do this by double-clicking the 'Home' button to obtain a screen similar to that of Fig. 5.1 on the previous page, then swipe each app in turn upwards to move it out of your screen, as shown in Fig. 5.2, which has the effect of closing the app. You'll be surprised how many apps are running on your device by the end of the day, so remember to close them frequently.

Fig. 5.2 Apps within a Folder.

Deleting an App

To delete an app, touch and hold on the app icon until it begins to wobble, as shown (static) here in Fig. 5.3, then tap the ⊗ icon that appears at the top-left of the app you want to delete, followed by clicking the 'Home' button to stop the wobbling.

Fig. 5.3 Deleting Apps.

> **Note:** It is worth noting that deleting an app, also deletes all data created by that app, so be careful what you delete.

Also note that certain apps, such as the **App Store** and **Wallet** shown in Fig. 5.3, to mention but the few, cannot be deleted as they are part of the iOS. In addition, apps within a folder cannot be deleted unless you first tap on the folder to open it, then touch gently the app you want to delete to make it wobble, then tap the ⊗ icon to delete it.

Scrolling within an App Screen

To scroll within an app screen such as, say, the **BBC News**, place your finger on the screen of the open app and drag it up or down to display more topics. If you swipe instead, scrolling is speeded up.

Some apps, such as the **Kindle** or **Books**, used to read a book, require you to move your finger from right to left to go to the next page, or left to right to go to the previous page of the book.

In other apps, such as **Photos**, depending on how your photos are grouped, you might have to move your finger on the screen up or down, left or right, to scroll through them. More about this shortly.

Using Folders on the Home Screen

First, touch and hold an icon on the 'Home' screen so that icons start to wobble, then select an icon and drag it onto another icon (usually of the same theme, such as **BBC iPlayer** and **ITV Player**). The iPhone creates automatically a new folder and gives it an appropriate name. Try it with any two apps on your iPhone. Those apps will then be kept within the newly formed folder.

As an example, have a look at the folder named 'Television', in Fig. 5.3 on the previous page, also shown here. It seems to me that apps serving similar functions can be held within a suitably named folder, so anyone of them can be found easily, rather than having to scroll thought endless 'Home' pages trying to find the one of interest to you at the time.

Here, I have placed all the apps relating to television in one folder. Now, some people say that the apps within such a folder are too small to distinguish them, so they dismiss the use of folders, but surely the caption is large enough to see what apps the folder contains! Then all you have to do is tap on the folder to expand it so you can easily see the individual apps in it, as discussed next.

Tapping a folder displays its contents, large enough for anyone to see the individual app icons held in it, as shown in Fig. 5.4.

To delete an individual app within a folder, tap the folder to open it, then touch the app gently with your finger until it causes them to wobble, then tap the ⓧ icon that appears at the top-left of the app you want to delete, followed by clicking the 'Home' button to stop the wobbling.

How many apps or folders you can accommodate per 'Home' screen (you can have more than one), depends on the size of your iPhone's screen.

Fig. 5.4 Apps within a Folder.

Organising New Apps

The total number of apps or folders that can be held on my iPhone, per 'Home' screen is 24 with each folder holding up to 9 apps. However, to be able to move apps or folders from one screen to another easily, it is a good idea to limit this number to one less than the maximum (23 in my case). The reason for this will become apparent soon.

In addition, the 'Dock' area at the bottom of the 'Home' screen, which is common to all 'Home' screens, can hold (in my case) 4 apps that I use more often. As this depends on the size of your iPhone's screen, don't be surprised if in your case this is different.

Any additional Apps you download, once the first 'Home' screen is almost full, are automatically downloaded on the next available 'Home' screen. To move a newly downloaded app into an existing folder which might be, say, on the first 'Home' screen, you'll first have to move it there, as follows:

- Touch the app you want to move. This will cause all apps to wobble.

- Next, touch the app you want to move again and very slowly drag it left to the previous 'Home' screen, then lift your finger off the app.

- If you are very careful, the app will occupy the free space you reserved on the previous 'Home' screen. But if your are not quick enough to lift your finger off the app, it might go further to the left on earlier 'Home' screens.

The procedure is the same when you try to move an app from, say, the first 'Home' screen to the second 'Home' screen, and so on.

Updating Apps

On earlier iOS versions, apps had to be updated manually. If you have such an early iOS you would notice a red numeral at the top-right of the 'App Store' icon, which when tapped would display a screen of all the purchased apps that need to be updated, with an explanation why that should be carried out.

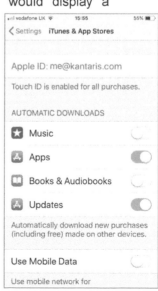

However, with later versions of the iOS, updates of apps are automatic, but make sure that 'Apps' and 'Updates' are switched on by going to **Settings**, then scrolling down to 'iTunes & App Store', as shown in Fig. 5.5. Here the buttons are shown as on. If, however, the buttons are not on, slide each to the right to turn them on.

Fig. 5.5 The iTunes & App Stores Screen.

Updating the Operating System

Occasionally you'll see a number against the **Settings** app, as shown here. This indicates that either there is an Operating System update or that you need to backup your system.

For the former case, tapping the app, displays the latest 'Software Update' (iOS13). For further information on iOS13, please refer to Appendix A.

Fig. 5.6 The Software Update Screen.

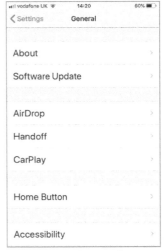

Fig. 5.7 The General Screen.

You could check your current iOS by tapping on **Settings**, then 'General' to display Fig. 5.7. Now tap on the 'About' option to get information on your iPhone, the 'Software Version' installed, together with the iPhone 'Model Name', 'Model Number', 'Serial Number', etc.

If you tap 'Software Update', it will check for an update and let you know if one is required. For an iPhone older than SE, the latest update will not be offered, although you will be told which version of the iOS you have. For an iPhone SE and later, you will be advised to upgrade to iOS13.

Customising the iPhone's Screen

It is very easy to customise your iPhone to your liking. To do so, go to **Settings** and select 'Display & Brightness'. This displays a screen similar to that in Fig. 5.8, in which you can change manually the normal brightness of your screen, the size of the displayed text, etc.

If you have an iPhone that shows the option 'Raise to Wake', as shown in Fig. 5.8, make sure that it is switched to 'ON' so that the phone wakes up by simply raising it, rather than having to press the 'Home' button.

You can also control automatic changes in brightness with variation of light, using the option 'Night Shift'.

To choose a 'Wallpaper' picture to customise your iPhone's screen, go to **Settings** and select 'Wallpaper'. This displays a screen similar to that in Fig. 5.9.

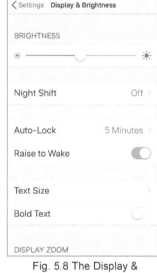

Fig. 5.8 The Display & Brightness Screen.

Dynamic wallpaper and perspective zoom are disabled when Low Power Mode is on.

Fig. 5.9 The Wallpaper Screen.

Tapping the 'Choose a New Wallpaper' option displays a choice of three built-In sets of wallpaper, as well as any photos you have taken with you iPhone, as shown Fig. 5.10 on the next page.

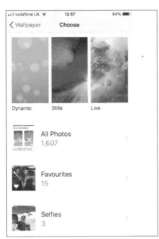

Fig. 5.10 Choosing a Wallpaper
Screen Set.

Tapping any one of the built-in sets, displays a choice of photos as shown in Fig. 5.11 for the 'Stills' set.

Fig. 5.11 The Stills Wallpaper Set
Photos.

Choosing one of these photos by tapping on the 'Set' button, you are given three options:

- Set Lock Screen
- Set Home Screen
- Set Both

Make sure that the design you choose for your 'Home' screen is as light as possible, otherwise you might find that it's difficult to see your apps. The photo you choose for your 'Lock' screen can be any as it only displays the time and date, so how dark the background is, has no effect.

Setting a Passcode to Lock the iPhone

By default, the iPhone does not require a passcode to unlock it. However, if you hold sensitive data in your iPhone, such as bank or personal details, that you do not want other people to have access to, if you loose your phone. Then you should set a passcode, so that only you can have access to it.

To set a passcode for pre iPhone 5, go to **Settings**, 'General', 'Passcode Lock' and tap the 'Turn Passcode On' bar at the top of the screen to set a four digit passcode.

For iPhone 5 and later, go to **Settings**, 'Touch ID & Passcode', scroll down and select option 'Turn Passcode On', at which point you'll be asked to supply a four number code, but with iOS 12.0 and later, you might be asked to enter a six number code.

It is worth spending some time scrolling through the 'Touch ID & Passcode' screen. For example, you could select to 'Use Touch ID' to unlock your iPhone and also to access several listed apps using your fingerprint. You will be asked to place your finger lightly on the 'Home' button (don't click it), so that your fingerprint can be read by the phone – you will be guided though the process.

If now you scroll to the very end of the 'Touch ID & Passcode' screen, you'll see the 'Erase Data' option. Activating this option, will erase all data on the iPhone after 10 failed passcode attempts. This is a precaution in case your iPhone is stolen and it holds sensitive data.

> **Note:** Do make sure you don't forget your passcode and/or loose your fingers, otherwise you will be in real trouble!

Using the iPhone to Search for Topics

If you swipe the screen to the right when on the first 'Home' screen the display changes to that in Fig. 5.12. You can use this screen to search your iPhone by typing in your query using the keyboard that displays when you tap the 'Search' bar.

Fig. 5.12 Searching the iPhone.

Speaking Assistant Siri

You could also use 'Siri', the built-in speaking assistant, directly to search for just about anything. For example, pressing the 'Home' button and holding it for a second or two, displays a screen with the message 'What can I help you with?', followed a second later with 'Go ahead I'm listening'.

You can, say, ask 'Siri' to convert pounds to grams, inches to centimetres or search for specific people or events. For 'Siri' to respond to voice commands, go to **Settings**, then 'Siri & Search' and turn on the first option in Fig. 5.13. A training session will follow to

Fig. 5.13 The Siri Options.

allow 'Siri' to get used to your voice. Now, you can just pick up the phone and say 'Hey Siri' which gets the response 'I'm here'. It can't be easier!

> **Note:** Upgrading to iOS13, causes 'Siri' to stop listening to voice commands until you turn off the 'Listen to Hey Siri', then turn it on again and go through the training process all over again.

6

Taking & Organising Photos

Taking photos with your iPhone is a very easy process, but unless you organise them into albums, you might find yourself spending hours trying to find a specific photo. This is the main topic of this chapter, though at the end of it I also discuss an easy way of transferring your photos from your PC to your iPhone and putting these into appropriate albums.

Taking Photos with an iPhone

The iPhone has two lenses; one at the front (refer to Fig. 1.1 on page 1), located 2 mm to the left of the built-in microphone with about 1 mm diameter and a much larger one at the back of it, as shown in Fig. 6.1. The white dot is a built-in flash, with the actual lens to the left of it.

The lens at the front of the iPhone is used to either take photos of oneself or to use with 'FaceTime' which is a phone call that allows both participants to see each other (more about these topics shortly).

Fig. 6.1 The Back of an iPhone.

The Camera App

There are two apps associated with photography; the **Camera** and the **Photos**, as shown in Fig. 6.2. Here they are shown within the **Photography** folder, but in your case they most likely will display separately.

Fig. 6.2 The Photography Apps.

So, to take a photo, tap on the **Camera** app to open it and point the back of the iPhone to an object, perhaps similar to the one shown in Fig. 6.3.

Fig. 6.3 Taking a Photo.

The object you are trying to photograph is displayed on the iPhone's screen. To take the photo, simply touch the white circular button that appears on your screen when in camera mode (called 'Take Picture' button). To stop the camera mode, press the 'Home' button.

At the top of the screen there are five options available here. From left to right, these are:

- 'Flash' and 'HDR' (High Dynamic Range), with 3 options each which display when tapped; 'Auto', 'On' or 'Off'. The default for both is 'Auto'.

- 'Live' (set to 'Off' here). This, when 'On', takes a series of photos (a kind of a mini video) which has the effect of animating your photos.

- 'Timer' with three options; 'Off' (the default), '3s' or '10s'.

- 'Filters' which when tapped, displays several options near the bottom of the photo screen as shown in Fig.6.4 (only the bottom of the screen is shown here), with 'Original' then several ranges within 'Vivid', 'Dramatic' and finally 'Silvertone', 'Mono' and 'Noir', as shown in Fig. 6.4 (only the bottom part of which is shown here.

Fig. 6.4 Showing Available Filters.

At the bottom of the screen, there are two buttons displayed on either side of the 'Take Picture' button:

- To the left, the last photo you took is shown which when tapped displays all the photos taken with your iPhone and allowing you to scroll through them.

- To the right of the 'Take Picture' button, the 'Switch between cameras' button is displayed, also shown here. Tapping this button switches cameras from the back to the front, so you can take a photo of yourself.

At the bottom of the screen when in 'Camera' mode, you have six options for different types of photography (Fig. 6.5) with the active one displayed in yellow. All options can be seen by moving your finger on the left or right of the currently selected option.

TIME-LAPSE   SLO-MO   VIDEO   PHOTO   SQUARE   PANO

Fig. 6.5 Photographing Options.

When 'TIME-LAPSE', 'SLO-MO' or 'VIDEO' is selected the inner part of the 'Take Picture' button changes colour to red, but still round, as shown here. You'll have to tap this button to start recording, at which point the inner part of the 'Take Picture' button changes to a red square, as shown here, which you then tap to end the recording.

Fig. 6.6 Taking a Panoramic Photo.

When you select PANO, the iPhone display changes to what is shown in Fig. 6.6 (only the bottom-half of the screen is shown here).

As instructed, you must move the iPhone slowly as you photograph a panorama, but keeping the white arrow on the displayed horizontal line.

The result could look similar to that in Fig. 6.7. This is Padstow estuary in Cornwall taken by my steady hand, in case you are wondering!

Fig. 6.7 A Panoramic Picture.

I must admit that taking panoramic pictures can be taxing. Not only must you scan the view at a constant rate, but you must do it while you keep the white arrow on the line provided, otherwise the photo might be inclined, out of focus or both!

You need to take a few photos so that you can follow what comes next which is putting photos into albums, as this will save you time when searching for a specific photo later.

Displaying iPhone Photos

The second app associated with photography is **Photos**, as shown in Fig. 6.8. Here it is shown within the **Photography** folder, but in your case it most likely will display separately.

The Photo App

To look at your iPhone pictures,

tap the **Photos** app, to automatically display the last photo you took, which, in my case, is the panoramic picture shown in Fig. 6.9. Note the additional options that show at the top-right of the display. Tapping the actual picture once, removes these options and displays the

Fig. 6.8 The Photography Apps.

picture as shown in Fig. 6.7 on the previous page. Tapping the picture once again toggles the options back again.

However, the position of the various options on the screen, depends on the orientation of the iPhone, as shown in Fig. 6.10 on the next page.

Fig. 6.9 A View of the Last Picture in 'All Photos'.

As you can see in both orientations of the iPhone, the same options are present, but are displayed in different places – for the portrait orientation, three of these:

Send

Favourites   ♡

Delete   🗑

are now displayed at the bottom of the screen.

Tapping the 'Favourites' option, places the picture into a special album called 'Favourites'.

Fig. 6.10 Position of Options.

Actually, all your photos are placed into an album called 'All Photos' but you can create additional albums to hold specific photos that belong to a given collection or have the same theme.

The 'Edit' option displays a screen with tools for editing, both at the top and bottom of the screen, as shown in Fig. 6.11.

Top

Bottom

Fig. 6.11 Editing Tools.

At the top of the screen you have tools for 'Redeye Correction' on the left and 'Auto-enhance' on the right.

At the bottom of the screen you have tools for 'cropping', 'Photo filters', 'Adjustments' to set 'Light', 'Colour' and 'B&W' and a 'Markup' tool. If you mess up your photo, use 'Revert'.

The blue left arrowhead < at the top-left of the screen (see Fig. 6.10 on the previous page), when tapped, displays 'My Albums'. So far, there should only be two albums; 'All Photos' and 'Favourites', as shown in Fig. 6.12.

Creating a New Album

To create a new album, tap the blue + icon at the top-left of the screen in Fig. 6.12. This opens a pane with three options, as shown in Fig. 6.13 below. Select 'New Album' to display a screen similar to that shown in Fig. 6.14.

Fig. 6.12 Albums.

Fig. 6.13 Selecting Type of Album.

Type a name for the new album, say 'Flowers', and tap the 'Save' button to create it and insert it into 'My Albums'.

Next tap 'All Photos' to display all your pictures, then tap the photos that represent your album name and tap 'Done'. This automatically places the selected photos into the newly created album.

Fig. 6.14 Naming a New Album.

If you start thinking that creating albums for just the 6 photos I used in the example is a waste of time, consider this:

In my collection, I have 1,623 photos and videos within 31 albums (at present), some of which are shown in Fig. 6.15. If it wasn't for the albums, imagine how long it would take to search for a specific photo!

Displaying Photos

There are several ways you can display and view your photos. For example, tapping the option 'Photos' at the bottom-left of the screen displays your photos in the year they were taken, as shown in Fig. 6.16.

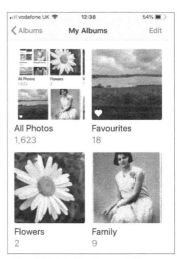

Fig. 6.15 My Photos and Albums.

Fig. 6.16 Displaying Photos by Year.

To see the photos within a certain year, tap on the actual photos of that year to display them within monthly dates of that year, as shown in Fig. 6.17.

Fig. 6.17 Displaying Photos by Monthly Dates.

Tapping again within a monthly period, displays the actual days that the photos were taken, as shown in Fig. 6.18.

Finally, tapping any individual photo, displays it in full screen, just as in 'All Photos'.

Each time you tap the blue arrowhead < at the top-left of the screen, it takes you back to the previous display.

Tapping the option 'For You' to the right of the 'Photos' option at the bottom of the screen displays photos as

Fig. 6.18 Displaying Dates Photos Were Taken.

'Memories' which, as expected, are dependant on your personal collection and perhaps you could look at them some time.

Deleting Albums and Photos

To delete an unwanted album, say 'Flowers', go to 'My Albums', tap on 'See All', then tap 'Edit' and tap the ● icon to remove it, as shown in Fig. 6.19.

Note the displayed message "Are you sure you want to delete the album 'Flowers'? The photos will not be deleted".

The reason for this is that photos in an album are not duplicates to those in 'All Photos', they are merely links, so the total space in the iCloud is not doubled by having albums. Note that the 'Favourites' album cannot be deleted – no ● icon displays on it.

Fig. 6.19 Deleting an Album.

> **Note:** Deleting individual photos in 'Favourites' will also remove them from 'All Photos'! If it happens by mistake, go to 'Albums' and scroll down to the 'Recently Deleted' album, locate the photo, 'Select' it and tap 'Recover'.

You can also follow the above procedure to recover any deleted photo from 'All Photos'.

Adding Photos to an Album

If you take a photo and you want to move it into an album, do the following:

Fig. 6.20 Selected Photo.

- Locate the photo in 'All Photos' and 'Select' it'. The lower part of your screen now changes to one similar to that in Fig. 6.20.

- Tap the 'Add To' icon to display all your albums.

- Tap the album you want the photo to be included in.

As the photo I chose for the example above is that of flowers, I naturally selected the 'Flowers' album.

Moving Photos from PC to iPhone

To move photos from your PC and make them availiable to the iPhone (via the iCloud), you need to refer to 'The iCloud Service on a Windows PC' on page 39 and must download iCloud for Windows, as discussed in that section which will allow your PC to get data from the iCloud and send data to it.

To recap, go to www.icloud.com, download the program, run it and restart your PC. Double-click the iCloud icon placed on your desktop, enter your 'Apple ID Verification Code' sent to your iPhone and sign in with your Apple ID to display the screen shown in Fig. 6.21 on the next page.

Fig. 6.21 The iCloud Screen on a Windows PC.

To transfer photos from the PC to the iCloud (so they become available on your iPhone), tap the 'Photos' icon on your PC to open a screen with all your photos and albums, similar to that of Fig. 6.22. I left-click the 'My Albums' to display them all as shown.

Next click the ⊕ icon to the right of 'My Albums' which only displays if your mouse is pointing to 'My Albums', to open a sub-menu asking you to chose between 'Create New Album' or 'New Folder', as shown on the left of Fig. 6.22.

Choose to 'Create New Album', which is created and gives you the opportunity to name it (in my case I call it 'Barcelona'. Next, locate all the photos on your PC associated with the newly create album and drag them across to it.

Fig. 6.22 The iCloud and PC Screens Side-by-side.

After a bit of time – it depends on the number of photos you are transferring to the iCloud, the screen changes to one similar to Fig. 6.23.

Fig. 6.23 The Contents of the New Album on iCloud.

I hope that you realise that describing this process takes a lot longer than actually carrying it out. It mostly depends how organised your photos are on your PC!

Renaming Albums on the iPhone

To rename an album on the iPhone:

- Return to 'Albums
- Tap 'See All'
- Tap 'Edit'
- Move insertion pointer to the label of the album
- Rename label
- Tap 'Done' at the bottom of the screen, then tap 'Done' again at the top of the screen.

7

More Apps, Control & Sharing

In this chapter, I discuss extra useful apps, some being part of the Operating System (iOS), the 'Control Centre' and extra 'Sharing' abilities which will help you master the iPhone's use.

The iPhone's Clock App

The iPhone's **Clock** app, shown here, can be used to set a
 timer, an alarm or to add clocks for different time zones which can be very useful if you have friends living in different places and you don't want to wake them up with your call!

Tapping on the **Clock** app opens the 'World Clock' screen similar to the one shown in Fig. 7.1, provided the same named option at the bottom-left of the screen is selected, as shown here.

Tapping the + icon at the top-right of the screen displays the 'Choose a City' screen shown in Fig. 7.2 on the next page. Note the letters of the alphabet to the right of the screen which, when tapped, take you directly to the cities starting with that letter.

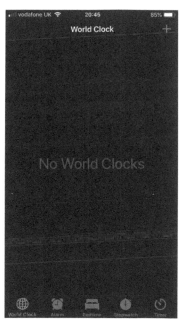

Fig. 7.1 The World Clock Screen on the iPhone.

This saves you scrolling through to find the city you are looking for. Having selected one city, you can then add further time zones, as shown in Fig. 7.3.

Fig. 7.3 Selected Cities.

Fig. 7.2 Choosing a City.

This is very useful to me; it stops me waking up my friends in the middle of the night which will make me extremely unpopular!

The second option from the left at the bottom of the **Clock** app allows you to set an 'Alarm', as shown in Fig. 7.4 – another excellent capability. You can even select the sound it makes, but sadly it does not provide you with a cup of tea!

Fig. 7.4 Adding an Alarm.

The third option at the bottom of the **Clock** app's screen, allows you to set up a recurring wake-up alarm after answering a few questions. It assumes you go to bed and wake up at the same time every day!

The fourth and fifth options of the **Clock** app's screen deal with setting a 'Stopwatch' and a 'Timer', respectively. I leave it to you to investigate.

Do Not Disturb Setting

I have discussed how to be considerate to your friends and avoid waking them up in the middle of the night with your call, but what about the other way around? Will your friends be as considerate as you? Perhaps it might be a good idea to make sure.

Tap the **Settings** app and scroll down to 'Do Not Disturb' option and tap it to open the screen similar to that in Fig. 7.5.

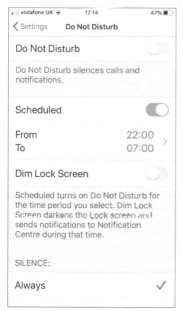

Fig. 7.5 The Do Not Disturb Screen.

Make sure that both 'Do Not Disturb' and 'Scheduled' options are turned 'On'. The second option then gives you the option to set the time period when you do not want to be disturbed by either calls or notifications.

I suggest you scroll down on the screen as there are lots of other options you can select. For example, you can allow calls from certain named individuals or those in your favourites list.

You could also allow repeated calls to reach you, in case you had an elderly person you worried about.

The Control Centre

To display and use the tools on the 'Control Centre', your iPhone must be unlocked first. A locked iPhone stops unauthorised persons having access to it.

Fig. 7.6 The Control Centre Panel Screen.

To access the 'Control Centre', touch with your finger the very bottom of the iPhone's screen (while holding the iPhone with the 'Home' button at the bottom of the device), and gently move your finger up the screen, to display what is shown in Fig. 7.6.

Some of the tools displayed here have been discussed already, but for the sake of completeness, I give a short description of each displayed icon.

 Airplane mode. When activated it changes colour to orange) and all connectivity is cut off – a requirement on take off and landing when in an aeroplane.

 When green, indicates that Internet data is 'On' – a requirement if you need to browse the Internet when away from a WiFi connection.

 When blue, indicates that the WiFi is 'On'. Tap it to disconnect.

 When blue, indicates that Bluetooth is 'On'. Tap it to disconnect.

Now playing box. This could be 'Music' or a 'News' voice commentary if you happen to be watching a video on the Apple 'News' app. Touching and holding the icon, displays a larger window where you can control the volume.

Orientation Lock. Tapping the icon turns it white and changes the middle of it to red, locking the iPhone into 'Portrait' orientation, unless it is overridden by an app.

'Do Not Disturb'. Tapping the icon turns it white with a purple half-moon and blocks calls, alerts and notifications.

Screen Mirroring. Tapping this icon, mirrors your screen to a compatible air enabled Apple TV which gives you a larger display.

Change the Brightness of the iPhone's screen. Slide the dividing line downwards to make screen less bright.

Change the Volume of the iPhone's speakers. Slide the dividing line upwards to increase the volume.

Flashlight. Tap this icon to turn your iPhone into a torch. Tap it again to turn it off.

Timer. Tap the Timer to display another screen from which you can reach the 'World Clock', 'Add Alarm', etc.

Calculator. Tap it to display a simple, but effective, calculator.

Camera. Tap it to launch the 'Camera' app.

 Favourite accessories will show up when you add them in the 'Home' app. Tap the 'Home' app to get information on what you can do with it, but you need access to iCloud and must be running iOS10 or later.

 Find a code to scan (new to iOS13)

Maps and Navigation

 Apple Maps (**Maps** for short) help you to see a 2D view of the world both in map and satellite image format. You can use **Maps** to search for locations and addresses, find local services or get directions to a specified location.

Tapping the **Maps** App, opens a screen asking your permission to find your location. After giving that permission, the screen changes to a display similar to the one shown in Fig. 7.7, but with an appropriate map for your area and your location pinpointed with a pulsating blue dot.

Note the box under the map, labelled 'Search for a place or address'. Tapping it displays the on-screen keyboard so you can enter information.

Fig. 7.7 The Opening Screen for your Location in Maps.

Searching for a Location

To see some startling views, search for 'St Ives Cornwall' or a location of your own choice. What was displayed in my case, is shown in Fig. 7.8.

Tapping the 'Directions' box, displays a road map with information on how to get there from your current location, how long it will take, etc., as shown in Fig. 7.9.

Fig. 7.8 A Location in Map View.

Fig. 7.9 A Selected Location.

Tapping the green 'GO' icon that displays, starts voice instructions on how to get there. Note that at the bottom of the screen in Fig. 7.9 the 'Drive' option is highlighted. There are other options available, however, namely 'Walk', 'Transport' and 'Ride', so you can find your way around easily even when walking in an unfamiliar place or city. Also note the two buttons near the top-right of the display in Fig. 7.9, also shown here.

Tapping the top button, displays the 'Map Settings' and allows you to select between 'Map', 'Transport' or 'Satellite', while the bottom button changes the orientation of the map.

Finally, revert to 'Location in Map View' (Fig. 7.8 on the previous page), tap the 'Info' button, and select 'Satellite' view, then tapping the 'x' button to clear the 'Map Settings' from the screen, displays Fig. 7.10 in which I have zoomed in to get a closer view of the famous beaches.

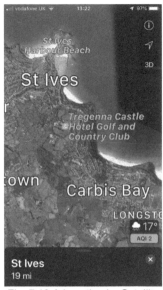

No matter where you are in the country, you can use **Maps** to find the nearest educational or amusement services. Enter the appropriate search criteria, followed by the words 'in' or 'near', and the town, city or other location in the 'Search' box.

For specific addresses, entering information in the 'Search' box in the form of 'Address', 'town' and 'post code' usually gives the best results.

Fig. 7.10 A Location in Satellite View.

Perhaps it might be worthwhile spending some time here to see the effect of all the available options – far too many to give precise description of them all. Experimenting in this case is by far the best way of finding out for yourself.

Apple News

Apple News (or **News** for short) is an app that lets you read the latest news and has links to other news providers, like the 'Telegraph', 'Guardian', etc.

Tapping the **News** app, displays a screen similar to the one shown in Fig. 7.11 on the next page. Note the three options at the bottom of the screen, namely 'Today', 'Spotlight' and 'Following'.

What is shown here is when the 'Today' option is selected. Obviously what you see, will be different as you are accessing the news on a different day.

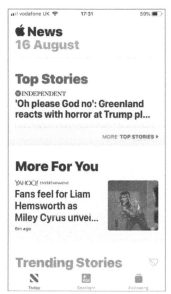

Selecting the second option, 'Spotlight' displays news similar to those in Fig. 7.12.

Fig. 7.11 Today's News.

Fig. 7.12 Spotlight News.

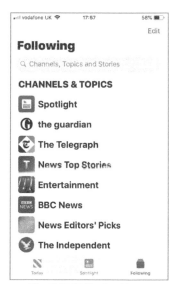

Obviously, what you see is bound to be different. but just in case you puzzle over the meaning of 'sapiosexual'; it means being attracted to similar intelligence!

Tapping the third option 'Following', displays a screen similar to that in Fig. 7.13, where you could edit the outlets you follow.

Fig. 7.13 Following News.

The Notes App

The Apple 'Notes' app is normally underrated by users, yet it can be very useful indeed.

You can use 'Notes' to keep lists of information, such as your National Insurance number, expiry dates of medication, labels of photos, type of engine oil for your car and anything else that you would like to access quickly, as shown in Fig. 7.14.

To delete an item from the list, tap it to open it, as shown in the foreshortened display in Fig. 7.15, then tap the 'Bin' at the bottom-left of the display. As you can see, this guarantee was only for a year and it is redundant by now.

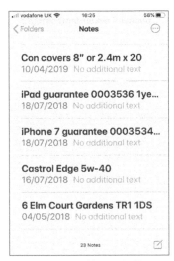

Fig. 7.14 List of Items in Notes.

Fig. 7.15 Deleting an Item from Notes.

I also tend to use 'Notes' to make a shopping list. Very convenient, as lists on paper tend to be left behind or lost on the way to the supermarket!

If a list in 'Notes' is important to you, make sure that it is kept on the 'iCloud' by going to **Settings**, then scrolling down to 'Notes' and selecting 'iCloud'.

Deleted items in 'Notes' go into a 'Recently Deleted' folder and can be retrieved, as follows:

When you tap the 'Notes' app, having deleted items from the list, you see a display similar to that in Fig. 7.16.

Fig. 7.16 Initial Display when Tapping the Notes App.

Next, tap the 'Recently Deleted folder to display its contents then tap the one list you would like to retrieve, to display the screen in 7.17.

Tapping the 'Recover' Option, transfers the selected list into the 'Notes' folder.

To remove items from the 'Recently Deleted' list, for pre-iOS13 users tap 'Edit', while iOS13 users, tap the 'More Options' icon at the top-right of the screen, shown here and in Fig. 7.18.

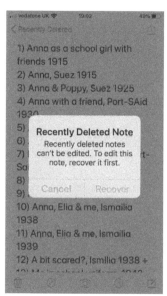

Fig. 7.17 List Item in Recently Deleted Note.

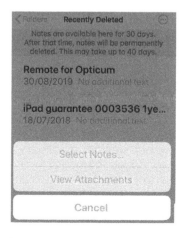

Fig. 7.18 Removing Items from the Recently Deleted Folder.

Selecting the option 'Select Notes' allows you to delete individual or all 'items from the 'Recently Deleted' folder.

Sharing Links, Albums and Contacts

To illustrate what happens when you receive a link by either e-mail or text, I will do so by sending them to myself. This will stop other people being involved and being inconvenienced.

Receiving a Link in an E-mail or Text Message

I have just sent an e-mail with a link to myself, but it did not arrive in my 'Inbox'. Instead, I found it in my 'Junk' folder, as shown in Fig. 7.19. This is why you should look at your 'Junk' folder occasionally, to see if anything has been placed there by mistake. **Mail** assumed that this particular e-mail was junk, as it contained a link to a Website which is trying to sell me something that I might not, want. Fig. 7.19 shows the contents of my 'Junk' folder.

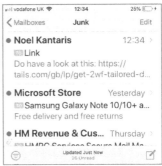

Fig. 7.19 The Junk Folder.

Please note the last e-mail in the 'Junk' folder – a good time to warn you that HM Revenue & Customs do not send out e-mail messages. The people who sent this e-mail, pretend that you were overcharged in your last tax return and that you are owed money. They then ask for your bank details so as to refund you! I don't need to tell you what will happen if you answer them.

To recover a genuine e-mail from the 'Junk' folder, tap it to open it, then tap the 'Folder' option at the bottom of the screen, shown in Fig. 7.20 which displays all your e-mail folders, then tap the 'Inbox'.

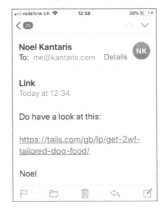

Fig. 7.20 Recovering an E-mail
From the Junk Folder.

Fig. 7.21 shows the same link received in a text message. Tapping either the link in the e-mail or the one in the text message, displays the result, as shown in Fig. 7.22.

Fig. 7.21 A Link Received in a Text Message.

Fig. 7.22 The Result of Tapping the Received Link.

Sending a Link by E-mail or Text Message

Assume you were browsing the Internet and found a Website that you think your friend should know about. For simplicity, I'll use the same Website as that shown in Fig. 7.22, namely www.tails.com. Typing this in **Safari**, displays the Website.

Next, tap the entry 'tails.com' at the top of the Website to

reveal the site's URL (Uniform Resource Locator). Now tapping the URL, displays a menu, as shown here.

Tap the 'Copy' option, then in the body of an e-mail or text message touch the screen to display a similar menu. Tap the 'Paste' option to copy the URL into your message.

Sharing Photos with Shared Albums

To share an album with a person whether in your **Contacts** or not, do the following: Go to **Settings**, 'Photos' and make sure that 'iCloud Photos' and 'Shared Albums' are turned 'On'.

- Tap the **Photo** app, then tap the album you want to share.

- Tap the 'Select' button at the top right of the screen, then tap the photos you want to share.

- Tap the 'Send' [⬆] icon and scroll to the right.

- Scroll to the right (5th option after 'Messages') and tap the 'Shared Albums' icon shown here.

- In the displayed iCloud screen, give the album a name and tap 'Next' at the top-right of the screen.

- Select the people you want to see this album by e-mail or mobile phone number.

- Provide an optional 'Comment', then tap 'Post'.

If you look at your albums now, you'll find the original album and a 'Shared Album'.

- Tap on the 'Shared Albums' to display the photos in it.

- Tap 'People' at the bottom of the screen to display a screen in which you can add people you want to include in sharing your album.

- If one of these people doesn't have an iPhone or doesn't have access to iCloud, then turn the option 'Public Website' to 'On' to include a provided link to the shared album, as shown in Fig. 7.23.

Fig. 7.23 A Shared Link.

To delete a shared album, tap the 'See All' option against 'Shared Albums', then tap 'Edit' and tap the ● icon of the album you want to remove. Selecting 'Delete', removes the album from your devices and from those of your subscribers.

Sharing a Contact's Information

Sometimes you might be asked to send a friend the phone number, e-mail address or both, of someone in your 'Contacts' list.

In this example, I have asked a friend to send me information about 'Babani Books'. This allows you to see both what is sent and what is received.

To send me this information, my friend would have to tap on his **Contacts** app, scroll down to find the specific contact shown in Fig. 7.24.

As you can see at the bottom of my friend's screen, there is an option to share this by selecting 'Share Contact'.

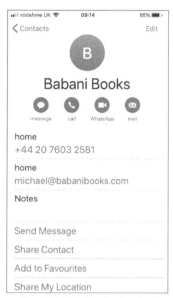

Fig. 7.24 Details of a Contact.

Fig. 7.25 Sharing a Contact.

My friend's screen will now display what is shown in Fig. 7.25. He can choose to send the information by 'Mail' or 'Message'.

If my friend selects e-mail, what I receive is shown in Fig. 7.26 on the next page. On the other hand, if he selected to send it by text message, what I receive is shown in Fig. 7.27, also on the next page.

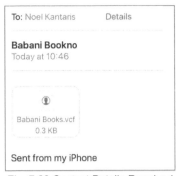

Fig. 7.27 Contact Details
Received by Text Message.

Fig. 7.26 Contact Details Received
by E-mail.

So by whichever method I receive this information, tapping on either link, opens a screen similar to that in Fig. 7.24 on the previous page, but with additional options at the bottom to 'Create New Contact', 'Add to Existing Contact' or 'Update Contact'. It is as simple as that!

Sending or Receiving Data via AirDrop

If two iPhones are near to each other, data such as photos or contacts can be sent from one iPhone to the other using 'AirDrop'. For this to succeed, both iPhones must be set to allow AirDrop to send and receive information.

Go to **Settings**, 'General' then select 'AirDrop' to display a screen similar to Fig. 7.28. Then tap 'Everyone' to select it on both iPhones.

Finally, choose the data you want to share (for a contact, use 'Share Contact'; for a photo use 'Select') and tap the option AirDrop shown in Fig. 7.25 on the previous page. The recipient has to accept. It can't be simpler!

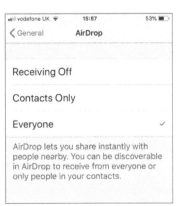

Fig. 7.28 AirDrop Options.

8

Extra Useful Apps

Although the apps to be discussed here are not standard Apple apps, they are extremely useful and you'll need to download them from the Apple Store.

The WhatsApp

The 'WhatsApp' is just about the most used app, not only on

 the iPhone, but on Android mobile phones. It is a free app and allows you to communicate using text or phone calls to anyone who has the app on their mobile phone, **anywhere in the world for free**.

 To obtain 'WhatsApp', tap on the 'Apple Store' app (shown here) and search for 'whatsapp'. From the displayed list of apps, select the 'WhatsApp for iPhone Free', which then displays a screen similar to that in Fig. 8.1. To download and install the app, tap the 'Get' icon on the 'WhatsApp Messenger' (the top entry in Fig. 8.1), unless you are in business, in which case select the second option which is not free.

Fig. 8.1 The WhatsApp Messenger.

Once the app is downloaded and installed on your iPhone, the 'Get' icon changes to 'Open' and tapping it, displays a series of screens, as follows:

- A Welcome to WhatsApp screen asking you to agree to their terms of service. Tap 'Agree & Continue'

- On the next screen, WhatsApp asks permission to send you 'Notifications'. Tap 'Allow'.

- On the next screen, you are asked to enter your iPhone number, using the on-screen numeric keypad, as shown in Fig. 8.2. When finished, tap 'Done'.

- On the next screen, you are asked to 'Restore' your chats (if any). Tap 'Skip Restore'.

- A screen similar to that in Fig. 8.3, is then displayed.

Fig. 8.2 Entering your iPhone Number.

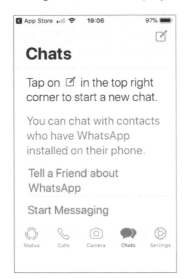

Fig. 8.3 The First Chats Screen.

Note the five icons at the bottom of Fig. 8.3. From left to right these are:

- 'Status'
- 'Calls'
- 'Camera'
- 'Chats'
- 'Settings'

Tap each in turn to see its functionality.

I leave it to you to explore these. In essence, sending or receiving a text using 'WhatsApp' is the same as sending or receiving a text using 'Messages' and using 'Calls' is similar to using the 'Phone' app, but both functions in 'WhatsApp' are free, even to mobiles in other countries!

The first time you tap the ☑ icon (top right in Fig. 8.3) to start a new chat, 'WhatsApp' asks permission to 'Access Your Contacts'. Tap 'Allow' to display all your 'Contacts' who have an account with 'WhatsApp'. If you include yourself in your contacts list, you can then experiment by sending a 'WhatsApp' message to yourself, as shown in Fig. 8.4 for my case.

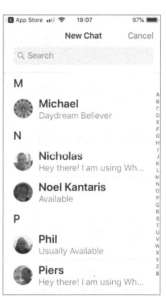

Fig. 8.4 My WhatsApp Contacts

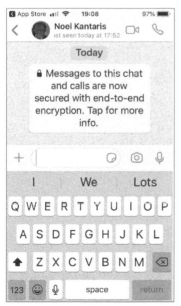

Fig. 8.5 The New Message Screen.

Every time you start a new message, to a new contact, the screen in Fig. 8.5 displays.

Note the message about encryption. What this means is, no one can intercept your messages or calls when using 'WhatsApp', unlike the built-in 'Messages' app or calls, using the 'Phone' app.

The BBC Weather App

Why use the BBC Weather app and not any of the many alternatives? Because it is easier to use, it is accurate and works where you are at the time, even abroad!

To get the app, go to the 'App Store' and search for 'bbc weather'. Select the app shown in Fig. 8.6 by tapping the 'Get'

icon. After downloading and installing it, tap the 'Open' icon that replaces the 'Get' icon.

Next, you are asked for your permission to access your location. Tap 'Allow'. A second screen then displays asking you whether you would like to 'See Alerts for UK Flood Warnings'. Tap 'Yes', which displays the screen in Fig. 8.7.

Fig. 8.6 Getting the BBC Weather App.

Note that the app displays the nearest weather station to you. Tapping the + 'Add' icon to the right of the location, displays the screen in Fig. 8.8 on the next page.

Fig. 8.7 The BBC Weather for My Location.

This screen allows you to

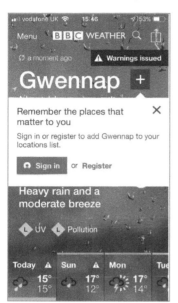

Fig. 8.8 Signing or Registering to a BBC Account.

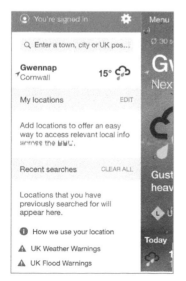

Fig. 8.9 Saved Locations.

'Sign in' (if you have already registered) or 'Register' if you haven't done so already.

Note that by registering, you can save locations that matter to you. So tap 'Register' to begin the process. You are asked for your date of birth, gender, Postcode, your e-mail address and asked to create a Password.

An e-mail is sent to you asking you to verify your e-mail address, after which you are asked to 'Sign in' with your credentials. Note that you are actually registering with the BBC, not just the 'Weather' app.

After signing in, tap on the 'Menu' (located to the left of the app header) to open the screen in Fig. 8.9. You can add more locations, by entering a location or postcode. This allows you to keep track of the weather at that location.

To remove an added location, tap it in the 'Menu' list to open its screen and then tap the ☑ icon against its name to turn it to ➕.

If now you touch the screen and gently slide your finger to the left, an hourly forecast is displayed as shown in Fig. 8.10.

As you can see, you'll have to wait until 6 p.m. before you can partly see the sun. I hope your weather forecast where you are is better than this!

Now, if you really want to be depressed, have a look at Fig. 8.11.

Fig. 8.10 The BBC Hourly Weather for My Location.

Fig. 8.11 A Weather Forecast Taken on the Island of Aegina.

I am making a point here. This weather forecast was taken in early September on the Aegean island of Aegina (see top-left of the screen which displays 'vf GR' for the service provider (in my case) 'vodaphone, Greece'. A screen dump was taken of the weather forecast at the time and sent to a friend in the UK via WhatsApp. Were you to search the 'BBC Weather' app for 'Aegina' in this country, the top-left of the screen would display (again in my case) 'vodafone UK'. This proves that the 'BBC Weather' app works abroad.

The BBC iPlayer

Another useful app is the 'iPlayer'. It allows you to catch up with many BBC programme channels' content, like series, documentaries, 'Box Sets', etc.

To get the 'BBC iPlayer' app, go to the 'App Store' and search for 'bbc iplayer'. You'll be asked to provide your Apple ID, before you can download and install it. When all is completed, tap the 'Open' icon or the app icon itself, shown here.

Next, your screen displays something similar to that in Fig. 8.12

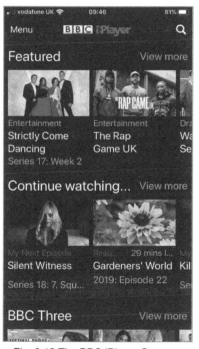

Obviously the content of the iPlayer screen will be different for you than the display here. I leave it to you to explore this app.

Needless to say that there are other apps that cover other TV channels, such as 'TVPlayer', 'ITV Hub', 'All 4' and 'My5'. The choice is yours!

If you are interested in current news from the BBC, you could also download and install the 'BBC News' app which provides you with free coverage, provided you have and declare that you have a TV licence!

Fig. 8.12 The BBC iPlayer Screen.

9

Appendix

Only the following iPhone devices can be upgraded to iOS13:

iPhone SE	iPhone X
iPhone 6s	iPhone XR
iPhone 6s Plus	iPhone XR Max
iPhone 7	iPhone XS
iPhone 8	iPhone XS Max
iPhone 8 Plus	iPhone 11

When you first upgrade to iOS13, the following information appears on your iPhone, then it vanishes. It is included here so that you can refer to it, explore and experiment at your leisure. When you have seen these new possibilities you might even be tempted to get one of the iPhones listed above.

iOS13 introduces a dramatic new look for the iPhone with Dark Mode, new ways to browse and edit photos, and a private new way to sign in to apps and Websites with just a tap. iOS13 is faster and more responsive with optimisations across the system that improve app launch, reduce app download sizes and make Face ID even faster. This update introduces new features and improvements:

Dark Mode:

• A beautiful new dark colour scheme that delivers a great viewing experience especially in low-light environments.

- Can be scheduled to turn on automatically at sunset, at a certain time, or turned on from the Control Centre.

- Four new system wallpapers that automatically switch appearances with Light and Dark Mode.

Camera & Photos:

- An all-new Photos tab with a managed view of your library, making it easy to find, relive and share your photos and videos.

- Powerful new photo editing tools that make it easier to edit, adjust and review photos at a glance.

- Video editing with over 30 new tools, including Rotate, Crop and Enhance.

- The ability to increase or decrease Portrait Lighting intensity on iPhone XR, iPhone XS, iPhone XS Max and iPhone 11.

- High-Key Light Mono, a new Portrait Lighting effect, for a monochromatic portrait with a white background on iPhone XR, iPhone XS, iPhone XS Max and iPhone 11.

Sign in with Apple:

- A private way to sign in to participating apps and Websites with the Apple ID you already have.

- Simple account set-up with only your name and e-mail address.

- Hide My E-mail to share a unique e-mail address that is automatically forwarded to you.

- Built-in two-factor authentication to protect your account.

- No tracking or profiling by Apple as you use your favourite apps.

App Store with Arcade:

- Unlimited access to groundbreaking new games with one subscription – no ads or additional purchases.

- An all-new Arcade tab in the App Store to browse the latest games, personalised recommendations and exclusive editorial content.

- Available to play across iPhone, iPod touch, iPad, Mac and Apple TV.

- Option to download large apps over your mobile data connection.

- Ability to view available app updates or delete apps from the Account page.

- Support for Arabic and Hebrew.

Maps:

- An all-new map rolling out in the US featuring wider road coverage, improved address precision, better support for pedestrians and more detailed land cover.

- Look Around to explore cities in a high-resolution, interactive 3D experience.

- Collections of the lists of places that you love and can easily be shared with friends and family.

- Favourites for quick and easy navigation to the places you visit daily.

- Real-time public transport, real-time flight updates and more natural spoken turn-by-turn directions.

Reminders:

- All-new design with more powerful and intelligent ways to create and organise reminders.

- Quick toolbar to add dates, locations, flags, attachments and more to reminders.

- New smart lists – Today, Scheduled, Flagged and All – to easily keep track of upcoming reminders.

- Sub-tasks and grouped lists to organise your reminders.

Siri:

- Personalised Siri Suggestions in Apple Podcasts, Safari and Maps.

- Over 100,000 live radio stations from around the world available with Siri.

- Shortcuts app now built-in.

Memoji and Messages:

- New Memoji customisation options including new hairstyles, headgear, makeup and piercings.

- Memoji sticker packs in Messages, Mail and third-party apps available on all iPhone models.

- Your name and photo, or even Memoji, now optionally shared with your friends.

- Search enhancements to easily find messages with intelligent suggestions and categorisation of results.

CarPlay:

- All-new CarPlay Dashboard with your tunes, turns and smart Siri suggestions on one screen.

- All-new Calendar app with a view of your day, option to drive to or dial in to meetings, and contact meeting organisers.

- Apple Maps redesign with Favourites, Collections and Road Junction View for China.

- Apple Music album art to easily find your favourite song.

- Do Not Disturb While Driving now available in CarPlay.

Augmented Reality:

- People Occlusion for apps to place virtual objects naturally in front of or behind people using iPhone XR, iPhone XS, iPhone XS Max and iPhone 11.

- Motion Capture for apps to understand the body position and movement of a person so you can animate a character or interact with virtual objects using iPhone XR, iPhone XS, iPhone XS Max and iPhone 11.

- Multiple face tracking for AR content on up to three faces at a time so you can have fun with your friends using iPhone XR, iPhone XS, iPhone XS Max and iPhone 11.

- AR Quick Look to view and interact with multiple AR objects at the same time.

Mail:

- Block sender to move all e-mail messages from a blocked sender directly to the Bin.

- Mute thread to stop notifications from an overly active e-mail thread.

- Format bar with easy access to rich text formatting tools and attachments of all kinds.

- Font support for all system fonts, as well as new fonts you download from the App Store.

Notes:

- Gallery view with your notes as visual thumbnails to help you find the note you need.

- Shared folders to collaborate with others, giving them access to entire folders of notes.

- More powerful search for visual recognition of images inside your notes and text in items you've scanned.

- New checklist options to easily reorder checklist items, indent them or move ticked items to the bottom of the list automatically.

Safari:

- Updated start page with favourites, frequently visited and most recently visited Websites, and Siri suggestions.

- View options in the Smart Search field for quick access to text size controls, Reader view and per-site settings.

- Per-site settings to choose Reader view, and enable content blockers, camera, microphone and location access for individual Websites.

- Download manager.

QuickPath:

- Slide to type on the keyboard for easier one-handed typing when you're on the go.

- Slide or tap to type interchangeably, even mid-sentence.

- Alternative word options in the predictive bar.

Text Editing:

- Scroll bar scrubbing to directly drag the scroll bar for quickly navigating long documents, web pages and e-mail conversations.

- Faster and more precise cursor navigation – just pick it up and move it to where you want.

- Text selection improvements for easier selection by just tapping and swiping on the text.

Fonts:

- Custom fonts are available from the App Store for use in your favourite apps.

- Font management in Settings.

Files:

- External drives supported in Files to access and manage files on a USB drive, SD card or hard drive.

- SMB support to connect to a server at work or a home PC.

- Local storage for creating folders on the local drive and adding your favourite files.

- Zip and Unzip support for creating and expanding Zip files.

Health:

- New Summary view of personalised data, including alerts, favourites, and relevant highlights from frequently used apps and devices.

- Highlights of health data from frequently used apps and devices showing trends over time in helpful charts and graphs.

- Cycle Tracking feature to log information about your menstrual cycle including flow level, symptoms and fertility metrics.

- Hearing health data types for environmental audio levels from the Noise app on Apple Watch, headphone audio levels and audio-grams from hearing tests.

Apple Music:

- Time-synced lyrics make listening more fun with perfectly timed lyrics.

- Over 100,000 live radio stations from around the world.

Screen Time:

- 30-day usage data to compare Screen Time numbers over the previous weeks.

- Combined limits to include multiple app categories, specific apps or Websites in one limit.

- "One more minute" option to quickly save your work or log out of a game when a Screen Time limit is met.

Privacy and Security:

- Allow Once location permission with the option to share your locations with apps only once.

- Background tracking alerts now notify you when an app is using your location in the background.

- Wi-Fi and Bluetooth enhancements help prevent apps from accessing your location without your consent.

- Location sharing controls give you the option to easily omit location data when sharing photos.

System Experience:

- Wi-Fi networks and Bluetooth accessories selection in Control Centre.

- A redesigned, volume control in the upper-left corner.

- Full-page screen-shots for web pages, Mail messages, iWork documents and Maps.

- Redesigned share sheet with intelligent suggestions to share content with just a few taps.

- Dolby Atmos playback for a thrilling surround sound experience from content with Dolby Atmos, Dolby Digital or Dolby Digital Plus soundtracks on iPhone XR, iPhone XS, iPhone XS Max and iPhone 11.

Language Support:

- Support for 38 new keyboard languages.

- Predictive input in Cantonese, Dutch, Hindi (Latin) Hindi (Devanagari), Najdi Arabic, Swedish and Vietnamese keyboards.

- Separate emoji and globe keys make it easier to quickly switch between languages and select emoji on iPhone X and later.

- Automatic language detection for dictation.

- Bilingual dictionary support in Thai and English and Vietnamese and English.

China:

- A dedicated QR code mode in Camera, accessible from the Control Centre, for improved QR code performance, a torch option and enhanced privacy.

- Junction View in Maps for drivers in China to more easily navigate complex roadways.

- Adjustable handwriting area on the Chinese keyboard.

- Cantonese predictions on the Cangjie, Sucheng, Stroke and Handwriting keyboards.

India:

- All-new Indian English male and female Siri voices.
- Support for all 22 official Indian languages with the addition of 15 new keyboard languages.
- Bilingual keyboard for Hindi (Latin) and English keyboard, including typing predictions.
- Typing predictions on the Hindi (Devanagari) keyboard.
- New Indian language system fonts for Gujarati, Gurmukhi, Kannada and Odia for greater clarity and ease when reading in apps.
- 30 new document fonts for Assamese, Bangla, Gujarati, Hindi, Kannada, Malayalam, Marathi, Nepali, Odia, Punjabi, Sanskrit, Tamil, Telugu and Urdu.
- Contacts with hundreds of new relationship labels to help more accurately label your contacts.

Performance:

- Up to 2x faster app launch.
- Up to 30 per cent faster Face ID unlocking on iPhone X, iPhone XR, iPhone XS, iPhone XS Max and iPhone 11.
- 60 per cent smaller app updates on average.
- Up to 50 per cent smaller apps from the App Store.

Other Features and Improvements:

- Silence unknown callers to get calls from known numbers in Contacts, Mail and Messages, while sending all other calls to voice mail.
- Optimised battery charging to slow the rate of battery ageing by reducing the time your iPhone spends fully charged.
- Low Data Mode to reduce your data usage over your mobile network or specific Wi-Fi networks you select.

- PlayStation 4 and Xbox Wireless Controller support.

- Find My iPhone and Find My Friends combined into a single app with the ability to locate a missing device even if it can't connect to a Wi-Fi or mobile network.

- Apple Books reading goals help make reading a daily habit.

- Calendar supports adding attachments to events.

- Family sharing hotspot for your family's devices to automatically connect to your nearby iPhone personal hotspot.

- Home app redesigned controls for HomeKit accessories with a combined view for ones with multiple services.

- Testing conducted by Apple in May 2019 using iPhone XS supporting normal peak performance, and iPad Pro (11-inch) with iOS12.3 and pre-release iPadOS and iOS13, using third-party apps repackaged in a pre-production App Store server environment; smaller app update download size based on averages from a collection of the most frequently updated apps. Performance varies based on specific configuration, content, battery health, usage, software versions and other factors.

- Testing conducted by Apple in May 2019 using iPhone X and iPhone XS Max supporting normal peak performance, and iPad Pro (11-inch) with iOS12.3 and pre-release iPadOS and iOS13, using the side or top button to wake the device. Performance varies based on specific configuration, content, battery health, usage and other factors.

Index

Notes

Notes